Breads, Cakes, Rolls & More *from Your* Bread Machine

Rob Wanless

Sterling Publishing Co., Inc.
New York

Library of Congress Cataloging-in-Publication Data

Wanless, Rob.
Breads, cakes, rolls & more from your bread machine / Rob Wanless.
p. cm.
Includes index.
ISBN 0-8069-6533-9
1. Bread. 2. Automatic bread machines. I. Title.

TX769.W285 1999
641.8´15 21--dc21

99-012501

10 9 8 7 6 5 4 3 2 1

Published by Sterling Publishing Company, Inc.
387 Park Avenue South, New York, N.Y. 10016
© 1999 by Rob Wanless
Distributed in Canada by Sterling Publishing
c/o Canadian Manda Group, One Atlantic Avenue, Suite 105
Toronto, Ontario, Canada M6K 3E7
Distributed in Great Britain and Europe by Cassell PLC
Wellington House, 125 Strand, London WC2R 0BB, England
Distributed in Australia by Capricorn Link (Australia) Pty Ltd.
P.O. Box 6651, Baulkham Hills, Business Centre, NSW 2153, Australia

Sterling ISBN 0-8069-6533-9

CONTENTS

The Reason for This Book

What! Still another bread machine book?" Well, yes, actually. And let me tell you how this one came about. I've only been writing recipes for others for a few years, but I've been cooking for over fifty years. My wife and I began writing down recipes for our kids after they moved out. We were getting phone calls from them asking how to make the things they remembered. Now they wanted to make it themselves; you know, "homesick" cooking. We got so many calls that my wife finally decided that maybe we could reduce the phone bill by collecting all our old standbys into a cookbook and giving each of the kids a copy, so we wrote down how we made the various things they all loved. It was then that I realized what there was to preparing recipes.

Collecting recipes for the kids was harder for me because I realized that I was no longer *using* recipes, except maybe for a quick check for proportions, or a mystery spice, or just as a boost to flagging confidence. Have you ever been around one of those cooks who just starts whipping something up, adding a bit of this and a bit of that, until he or she comes up with something delicious? You ask what it is, or even what is in it, and invariably the answer is something like: "Oh, I don't know, it's just something I threw together." Brian Maynard, at KitchenAid, whose primary duty it seems is dealing with people who cook like this, refers to this as Zen cooking. I can't explain how it works; I don't think anyone can do that. I don't want to go into it philosophically, except to say this: with cooking (and I suppose this holds true with dressmaking, woodworking, music, painting, and all the arts), you (the artist) reach that point where you no longer think about it, but are suddenly just doing it.

To encourage you to bake bread like that was one of the purposes of my first book and is even more so the purpose of this one — simply to get you "just doing it" without really thinking about it, and, of course, to make it easy! You might say my goal is to get you cooking without recipes, which I'm sure is not one of the goals of cookbook authors in general. Of course, you are going to have to supply the "will to do" yourself. But that's where this little book comes in.

A Word or Two About the Bread Machine

The bread you make yourself using a bread machine — a wonderful, inexpensive little gadget — surpasses all but the best and most expensive breads baked by skilled bakers. And, incidentally, I believe that the bread machine has contributed to the excellent breads which are increasingly available in the "bakeries" in the larger chain grocery stores and in the growing number of small independent and franchised bakeries around the world.

However, the wonderful little bread machine, which at this writing has just started its second decade and is improving rapidly (and it was pretty good to start with), is not without its limitations, although even these limitations, I believe, will probably be overcome.

The limitation of the machine that troubles me most (more common with the machines that use the "vertical" type bread pan, as opposed to some of the newer ones, which use the more "horizontal" type pans) is this: as the bread gets higher in the final rise before baking, the upper part of the bread tends to be airy, while the lower part remains too dense. I believe that I have overcome this problem to some extent. I'll tell you how in the "tips" section following this.

Bread machines are at their best and most convenient when being used as dough makers. They save an awful lot of time and make it possible for any one of us to make bread and rolls, specialty things that are unobtainable except at better bakeries.

Bread machines are under constant development; what are at present limitations may shortly be corrected, perhaps even by the time you read this. There is, however, one "shortcoming" that may not be under development, and that is because the shortcoming is actually with us. Speaking to, or about, my fellow countrymen, Americans, and that includes me, this shortcoming has to do with time. We simply cannot take time. We're learning, of course, and our growing love of wine is teaching us something about time as the wonder ingredient in many things. As an example: while you can introduce some special ingredients to make a sourdough loaf, you do this to avoid taking the time to use the real thing. The time we are talking about by the way, is really only about 12 to 20 hours, while the yeast causes the fermentation of the sugars in the wheat. It is this fermentation which gives the loaf its beery taste. Well worth the wait, I say!

Although various bread machines have different niceties, such as warning beeps to tell you when to add the raisins, cooling fans, talking modules, and the like, they all seem to work more or less the same way, fortunately. As for the "fruit beeper," which beeps to tell you to add fruit or other things to the dough towards the end of mixing, one of my machines has it. If yours does, use it.

Tips for Better Bread Making

I can say with reasonable certainty that my recipes work in all of the bread machines. Here are several tips to make your bread machine baking a little easier, and the bread a little better.

1. My brilliant daughter Kirsten suggested this. Prepare a bread-baking environment. That's the way a college graduate from an expensive midwestern university says: make a place for your bread machine. An example for this is what Ron Kurtz, my brother-in-law, made: On a kitchen countertop, directly above one of those narrow drawer kitchen units, he has his bread machine. In the top drawer beneath the counter, is his flour supply. He looked around to find a plastic container which exactly fit in the drawer and was sufficiently large to hold at least 5 lbs of flour. The flour container fits back in the drawer, and in front of it is space enough for a couple of measuring cups, spoons, and the et ceteras necessary for his bread making. The space on the counter in front of the machine is large enough, just, for kneading dough. All this in a space of approximately 18 inches wide and 24 inches deep. This setup makes it possible to prepare a loaf of bread in your machine in about 2 or 3 minutes.

2. Get a cheap, lightweight, 2-cup aluminum measuring cup to keep in your flour canister.

3. Always scoop the flour into the measuring cup with a scooping spoon, instead of just scooping the measuring cup into the flour. There is a difference in the final measurement.

4. Learn to measure sugar and salt, the small quantities anyway, into your hand. You can do it. (Of course, you wash your hands first!)

5. When using tap water, especially in the winter, use the water from the hot spigot for warm water.

6. Note the time when the second, or last, rise begins. Some bread machine booklets are good about giving you a more or less accurate timing for each of the stages in the cycles. Here's why: Just before the last rise begins, the machine will knock the dough down and release the gas, but most machines only run this course for a minute. This is not enough time. The dough retains too much of the gas in the upper part of the loaf, so that when it rises for the last time before baking, the upper part retains too much gas, and when baked is too airy or light, or not consistent. As soon as this kneading stops, or within a minute or two of its stopping, remove the dough ball from the pan and knead it yourself. Press all the air out of it; this should only take another minute.

7. While the dough is out of the bread pan, remove the kneader paddle from the bottom of the pan. Now put a bit of oil or butter on the kneader shaft, and drop the dough ball back into the pan, and the pan into the machine. When the bread is done baking, you'll find have a loaf without the big odd hole from the kneader paddle — only a nice little one.

8. Keep in mind that the best bread is finished by hand.

9. When working at high altitudes (2500 feet or so up) reduce the yeast a bit, maybe even as much as a half teaspoonful. (But then, if you are living at those altitudes you probably already know that.)

A Brief Review of Ingredients

It is in the general stores in rural communities, where they cater to people shopping for larger quantities, who go for longer periods between shopping trips, that you find your best selection of the things we use, and often better prices. Larger cities, however, can boast of restaurant and institutional supply companies, many of which sell bakery items in bulk: flour, sugar, yeast, gluten, et cetera. Since these companies are a bit uncommon, and could conceivably be reticent about selling retail, you will have to check. Most of what I use in my breads is readily available at supermarkets, however.

The first, and most important, ingredients in bread are yeast, flour, water, and salt. Finding the varieties of these four most important things, excepting maybe salt, can require a bit of searching. Let's review these first four most common things, and give you some tips on saving money and improving the taste and the quality of what you're baking.

Yeast
This is the first and the most important ingredient, the one absolutely essential ingredient to make bread as we know it. Yeast is everywhere, even

in the air we breathe. It is a single-celled fungus, of genus saccharomyces. This particular strain, which is capable of fermenting carbohydrates, a prerequisite in making two of life's greatest gifts, bread and beer, has been around for several thousand years.

Rapid Rise Yeast: *All the recipes in this book are based on using rapid rise or quick rise, or instant yeast. If you are using regular dried yeast, you will have to add a bit more, perhaps as much as ½ teaspoon more, to the recipes.*

The technology that makes it possible for us to use this necessary little fungus is rather advanced. Hence those little one-use packets are a bit expensive. But yeast bought in 1-lb packages is quite inexpensive. A 1-lb bag of yeast lasts me a couple of months, and I bake a lot. What you do is buy one of those nice little 4-ounce, brown glass brand name jars of yeast (yes, I know they are bit pricey, costing more than twice what you pay for a 1-lb package of yeast, but they are a good little jar to keep bulk yeast at the ready in your refrigerator).

Here are some of the yeasts which are available all over. For domestic yeasts (US/Canada), there are Fleischmann's and Red Star. Then there is a French brand, SAF, produced in Belgium and Mexico. My current favorite is an Italian yeast, Fermipan, which I am able to buy at a local grocery store. But there are more, probably many more. For instance, Hodgson's Mills sells their own brand of yeast, which is quite good, but I have seen it only in single-serving packages (hence it is expensive). King Arthur's Catalog also offers a good yeast.

Aging of Yeast: When you buy your yeast in bulk, and if you bake a loaf of bread or batch of rolls nearly every day, a 1-lb package is going to last you nearly 3 months. After a couple of months, you may find the yeast not quite as active. You may have to increase the amount of yeast you are using.

Where do you get these 1-lb packages? I have seen the 1-lb packages in cash-and-carry stores connected with institutional supply places and of course in those better general stores, featuring foods in bulk.

Flour

I find it interesting to travel about, especially into the American southland, and observe the varieties of flour available in the better (rural) supermarkets there. In one Winn-Dixie store in southern Virginia, I counted nearly a dozen different brands of flour. They were, for the most part, regular all-purpose flour, but the fact that there was such a variety, all from mills within a couple of hundred miles of the store, said a lot. And what it speaks of is the way people are inclined to eat in the South. I know of a case where a Pennsylvania friend's mother (who lives in Georgia) came to visit. Picking her up at the airport, and carrying her luggage to the car, he commented on one particularly heavy bag. "That's my White Lily flour. You Yankees don't sell it," she replied. Right she was. If you're lucky enough to have access to the products of one of these excellent independent mills, use them. The great majority of us have to buy what's readily available. Fortunately, that's not bad news.

However, you might want to think about this if you are really a stickler for healthy bread. If you really want to do some interesting experimenting, if you want to capture the taste of bread from days gone by, you can always mill your own flour. I have the feeling, as I write this, that in 5 years' time what I'm suggesting will be quite commonplace. KitchenAid sells a mill for their larger mixer, and I have seen other mills advertised in catalogs, e.g., the King Arthur's Catalog. These mills are not cheap; considering what they do, it's no wonder. But compared to the junk that people spend their money on, a mill could prove to be a very wise thing to own. I have found that wheat berries are readily available, and what happens to the flavor of your bread, to say nothing of the nutritional value, is beyond measure. I just thought I'd add that paragraph for you to file away in the back of your mind. Just remember, you read it here first.

The main flours for the recipes in this book are wheat — white or whole wheat — and rye. You'll catch mention of potato, soy, corn, and buckwheat flours, but they are really nutritional or flavor additives.

White Wheat Flour: There are four types of white wheat flour that we can readily use in the bread machine, as follows:

1. **All-Purpose Flour** is your garden-variety, bleached, enriched, etc., everyday, store-bought white flour. It's a mixture of soft and hard wheat.

2. **Unbleached All-Purpose Flour** is white flour in which no bleaching agents have been used. It is slightly tan ("wheat-colored," you might say). It too is a mixture of soft and hard wheat. It seems a bit more granular than bleached all-purpose flour, and it makes excellent bread.

3. **Bread Flour** is usually bleached, bromated, enriched, et cetera, although there are unbleached bread flours available. Bread flour has a bit more protein and hard wheat in it, and by and large gives a better loaf of bread than all except high-gluten flour.

4. **High-Gluten Professional Baker's White Flour** is ground mostly from

hard winter wheat, is significantly higher in protein, and generally requires some type of machine to work it. It gives your loaves the quality for which you are probably looking.

Until recently, most of the time we used good ol' store brand all-purpose unbleached white flour in our bread machines. We thought the unbleached flour was probably a little healthier, as it did not have the chemicals need-ed to bleach, and all. It does seem to have more flavor than the regular all-purpose flour (but that may have been my imagination). We also use bread flour when it is sensibly priced. Bread flour usually costs at least about half again as much as all-purpose flour. It does seem to give a bit higher loaf (but not always), and sometimes a superior crumb.

Then I tried commercial or bakers' flour. I first learned about it from a baker who was talking about the flours he used. He said you couldn't work this type of flour at home. And you couldn't. It takes machine power to work it, and unless you had one of those big mixers, you were out of luck. But it seems the humble little bread machine by its very nature has what it takes to work this flour.

The people at King Arthur's Flour figured this out too, and used the information, wisely I might add, to sell their excellent unbleached "Bread Machine Flour." The folks at White Lily Flours have also known about it, for their bread flour works exceptionally well in a bread machine. I've con-firmed it and I'll pass this information along to you.

There are other high-gluten professional baker's flours. It takes a little effort to locate them, but it's worth it. The catch is you have to buy this flour from institutional supply companies. Depending upon where you buy it, it may be cheaper than buying bread flour in the grocery store. Both Pillsbury and General Mills have excellent professional flours. However, it comes in 25 or 50 lb sacks. The prices for these professional flours, at least in my area, are below what you pay for bread flour, and in some cases even below regular all-purpose flour. Since you can figure on a bag of this flour lasting you a couple of months, it might prove to be worth the inconven-ience of having to find a place to store it.

If you like to or have to save money and you haven't an institutional supply company nearby, keep your eye out for store brands of unbleached all-purpose flour or the usual late summer or winter seasonal flour sales, and buy in quantity. Flour can keep for a year, when well-sealed and in a cool and dry place.

There is one more white wheat flour I should mention, semolina. This is made of a hard wheat called durham wheat, and is most commonly used in pasta. It is a high-gluten flour. Some bakers are known to add up to ¼ cup of semolina to a 3 cup measurement for their pizza dough. So, if you have trouble finding gluten, but you can find semolina, use that. I've noticed that semolina is increasingly available in grocery stores, usually in the pasta section.

Whole Wheat Flour: Whole wheat flour is just regular wheat flour with the whole wheat kernels, or bran, not winnowed out, but ground right into the flour. Because the kernels are in with the flour, they cut the gluten strands so the dough doesn't rise as well, nor as quickly. The loaves from your machine will be a bit firmer and not as high as if you didn't use it. Usually what you do to compensate is add as much as 50% white flour to the dough; that helps it to rise nicely. Many bread machines have a whole wheat setting, which gives a longer time for the rising. If it still isn't satisfactory, you can do the loaf on the dough cycle, or even remove the dough from the machine before it starts to bake, finish the loaf by hand, and give it a third rise before baking. But if you want 100% whole wheat bread, all you have to do is add some gluten to the whole wheat flour.

You might want to add a little whole wheat flour to your regular white bread recipes; you'll not only add nutrition, but a nice bit of additional flavor. It's especially good when making sandwich breads for people carrying lunches to work or school.

Rye Flour: Rye is readily available, and is used to make rich, dense, savory and tasty loaves of bread. Ham on anything else simply doesn't make sense. Rye flour has a different type of gluten, which isn't as elastic as wheat gluten, so rye flour doesn't rise well. For good rye loaves, you need at least half wheat flour, preferably a bread flour, or some gluten to put in with it. There are several types of rye flour available; some regular-grind big-name commercial stuff, and some coarse-ground rye, like Hodgson's Mills' rye flour. Hodgson's isn't the only one that puts out a coarse-ground or pumpernickel flour. King Arthur's offers one also. I prefer this type of rye flour when trying to effect a Euroloaf or Old World flavor. Adding a couple of tablespoons of coarse-ground rye flour to French or Italian bread seems to give it a lighter crumb and a somewhat crisper crust.

Gluten: If you haven't any bread flour or similar high-gluten flour around and you've found that the standard all-purpose flour is unsatisfactory, you can buy pure gluten. This is a manufactured gluten, made from wheat or corn. Gluten will help supply the glutinous fibers that catch the gas the fermenting sugars produce, which helps the bread to rise. Gluten is particularly helpful when you are adding fruits or vegetables to your dough. You use approximately one tablespoon per 3 cups of flour. Do this and you'll find the loaf rises nicely, as well as having increased protein content. You should be able to find gluten in the grocery store, usually near the baking products.

Other Flours and Meals: Potato, rice, corn, and soy flour are used primarily as nutritional and flavor supplements. If you are ever using about a half cup or more of any of the three, you should add a little extra gluten, or bread flour, in with these flours; it gives the yeast something to push against.

The coarser flours or meals (cornmeal, oatmeal, graham flour, or bran) are like the above and make for some marvelous and tasty breads. The same holds true for these regarding adding bread flour our gluten-enriched flour.

Note: Always have a bag of cornmeal handy, for spreading on the baking sheets or griddles when making English muffins, or dinner rolls or baguettes.

Oatmeal, cooked cornmeal (as in polenta), and even leftover grits can be used in bread. I can't give you a formula to use, based, say, on the percentage of water to meal and the appropriate adjustment in flour and water in the bread dough. What I do, when I find one of these blessings awaiting me in the fridge, is just dump it in with a regular bread recipe. Naturally, I check the dough ball after 5 minutes or so, and add flour if the dough is too wet, or water if the dough seems too dry. With the oatmeal I recommend an extra tablespoon of sugar and ⅓ cup of raisins — for oatmeal-raisin bread.

Salt: A remarkable thing, salt. My trusty old *Encyclopedia Britannica* gives it a full 3 pages. And necessary! Bread without it comes close to being inedible. Salt is necessary in bread for more than just flavoring. Salt strengthens the gluten and restricts, or controls, the action of the yeast. Without it your bread has a loose texture that's not very nice (yuch!). Too much salt makes for a tight texture that is hard to cut and chew.

I read somewhere that the iodine in most commercial table salts interferes with, or actually harms, the development of the yeast, and that therefore it's a good idea to use salt without iodine. I'm not sure how true that is, but I use sea salt. First of all, I think it is saltier (it seems so to me). But I'm not a fanatic about it. I use what's available. I just try to make sure sea salt is always available. Table salt without iodine is also readily available.

Water: Recently we moved from a small city in the mountains of central

Pennsylvania, 130 miles east to the flatlands east of the Alleghenies and nearer sea level. In Altoona we had used the city water, which came from some reservoirs in the Alleghenies, up above the famous Horseshoe Curve. It was that water which I used in formulating many of my bread recipes. When we moved into the new house, which has well water, and we began baking bread here, suddenly the recipes that I had used for so long, the ones that had been checked by our friends and had been verified in other ways, were not coming out correctly. I felt the dough ball after it had been working for several minutes and discovered the dough was too wet, and further, this seemed to be the case in all my recipes. I was having to add anywhere from ¼ cup to ½ cup more flour. It seems it was the water!

I'm sure by now you know recipes using flour can only be approximate. Until recently, I had thought that was due to the vagaries of flour: age, protein content, hardness of the base flour, humidity, and a lot of et ceteras. While that is certainly true, I realize now that one must also consider the water. However, in dealing with water in your bread recipes, the water you use is most likely the water you will continue to use. So, fortunately, checking and correcting the amount of water you use is a one-time adjustment, which you probably can apply to your other recipes. This is why I suggest you check the dough ball in the machine after several minutes.

Milk: In addition to water, milk is the other popular liquefier. Most sweet-dough recipes suggest milk. It gives a nice, dense crumb, adds nutrition, and will even help preserve the loaf. Dry-milk solids can be substituted, but most of us have milk in the fridge, so why bother with the dry stuff? It's expensive and superfluous.

Juices: Orange juice is wonderful in fruit breads and other sweet breads, but cranberry or apple juice works well. Most liquid will not bother the yeast, and the sweeter liquid, with its extra natural sugar, will enhance the development of the yeast.

The ingredients panels of commercial breads often list ascorbic acid, or sometimes Vitamin C. Yeast likes vitamin C; moreover, it seems to like it straight. A nice shot of lemon juice does the trick. You'll find the yeast livelier, and the flavor enhanced, with the simple addition of maybe a teaspoon or so of lemon juice. This is especially true when making fruit breads or vegetable breads.

Potato Water: When you drain potatoes after boiling, save the cooking water to use in bread. If you aren't going to use it right away, keep a canning jar handy to pour the water into; then drop a top on it. When it cools, put it in the refrigerator. It usually seals and stays fresh. I heat it for a minute on high in the microwave, before putting it in the bread pan. Potato water enhances the flavor of the bread and changes the texture. Since potatoes are usually boiled in salted water, you may want to cut the amount of salt in the recipe when you use it. If there aren't any little potato bits on the bottom of the pan or jar, put a tablespoon of the potatoes in the water.

Shortening: Lard, butter, margarine, olive oil, vegetable oil, vegetable shortening, bacon fat, and suet are all shortenings. Shortening helps to give bread a smoother, denser texture, a somewhat more tender crumb and, because it helps retain moisture, shortening also acts as a preservative. It also makes dough easier to work with, which is important when you are using the dough setting and hand-kneading for the second rise. You do not need shortening to make a good loaf of bread, however.

If you read the nutritional panels on commercial loaves of bread, you'll find vegetable shortening the most common shortening. In the recipe books that come with bread machines, you find that butter or margarine seems to be the most recommended. Butter does good things for bread, adding flavor and texture. But in bread, as with pie crusts, you'll find "experts" (the serious cooks, not the ones pandering to the popular cooking trends) seem to agree that nothing beats lard. Yes, yes, I know: lard is still a baddy, pure old saturated animal fat. But even for those on low- or reduced-fat diets, there is hardly a significant amount of this shortening in the average loaf of bread to worry about. Lard is absorbed well by hard wheat flour and leaves a delightful residual flavor, something akin to a hint of good French fries.

My next-favorite shortening has become margarine — real corn-oil margarine. You have to be careful buying margarine. The oil content of real margarine is set by law. But those old reliable brands have changed their formulas and they are now called "spreads." They are no longer real margarine, so you can no longer substitute your old favorites for butter, as you used to be able to do. What you want to buy is some real corn-oil margarine. That you can substitute for butter or lard. However, it does change the texture.

About the Other Shortenings: Your best bets in avoiding odd residual flavors are either olive oil or corn oil. Olive oil tends to add a savory flavor, which distinguishes Italian bread and pizza dough. And I know of some bakers who insist that for "real" Vienna bread you must use corn oil. Of course, good old cooking oil does work well, and most probably you wouldn't notice any difference. It is, after all, just plain soybean oil.

For flavoring bread a bit, to make ham sandwiches with the bread, bacon fat is like lard, but adds more than a hint of bacon flavor. Another secret ingredient, which has long been known to enrich flavors, is suet — beef fat — rendered down, of course. If you have an accommodating butcher, get him to cut a bit of beef suet, a pound or two. Save some for the woodpeckers, nuthatches, and chickadees. Put half of it in a pan of water and, simmering it, render it for a couple of hours. Chill it, and remove and use what comes to the top. Use that fat for frying French fries and even in your bread. And, just in case the fat police come to investigate, you are only using a tablespoon or so in the average 1½- to 2-lb loaf of bread.

Sugar and Other Sweeteners: Yeast feeds on sugar; as it feeds, it ferments, generating gas, nice gas, carbon dioxide. The gluten in the dough is fibrous. The fibers hold the gas that develops, and that's what makes the bread rise. There are natural sugars in the wheat that the yeast feeds on also. But the yeast really likes the additional sugars, or sweeteners, and they act as preservatives! They also, it should go without saying, add to the flavor of the bread and to the color of the crust. All your sugars are going to contribute to a darker crust. Those great French or Italian loaves which have little or no sugar are very light in color — hence, they get egg washes to make them nice and golden brown. They are wonderful when fresh, but this freshness lasts only for, at the most, a day. In fact, that fresh texture and flavor begin to fade within a few hours.

Among the many sweeteners that can be used in bread are sugar, of course, regular good ol' refined cane sugar, or brown sugar, and fructose, which, while it isn't exactly cheap, works well with fruit bread; yeast loves to munch on it. When you use honey in sweet white breads, it leaves a hint of an almost flowery taste. **Note:** When you use honey, measure it with the liquids, so a bit more flour is usually required if you're substituting honey for sugar in a recipe. I like brown sugar in my dark breads.

Molasses takes the dark ingredients one step further and imparts a rich, almost husky flavor to dough. This is good for the darker concoctions, and helps toward a suitably dark pumpernickel bread.

Malt Syrup: You'll often find this listed on the ingredients panel of breads. At one time it was a regular on grocery store shelves. Of late I have found malt syrup only at health food stores, and in 1-lb jars. Malt syrup does more than the other sugars, by contributing to a stronger, crisper, crust. While you use it in the same quantity as regular sugars, it does seem a bit sweeter, and it's quite sticky. A prerequisite for making proper bagels.

Everything Else You Can Put Into Your Bread Dough

Eggs: One of my favorite breads is challah. I love not only the taste, but also its smell, which is better than that of any other bread when it's baking. It's eggs which add the slightly caky-tasting, stretchy texture and the higher nutritional value to challah.

When you use an egg in the recipe, keep in mind that it is about 75% water, so you measure it as part of the liquid ingredients. In the recipes, you'll see something like: "1 egg + water sufficient for 1 cup." To do this, put the egg into the measuring cup first. Beat it slightly; then add the other liquids to the desired cup level. Small or medium eggs are better than the larger ones (lower cholesterol and fat, higher flavor, etc.), but 9 out of 10 of us buy large eggs. In my last book, I suggested that you can use a small egg in the 1 lb bread machine recipe, a medium egg in the 1½ lb bread machine, and 2 smalls or an extra-large in the 2 lb bread machine recipe. I still think that is best — and forget about those jumbo eggs. Otherwise, if I'm making a smaller recipe and using large eggs, when I break the egg, I do it over the sink, and let a bit of the white spill out. I use what seems right at the time; it's a judgment call. There is one exception to this; I'll let you know when we get to my marvelous new recipe for challah.

Fruit: Raisins seem to stand up to the domineering flavor of wheat, which has a tendency to quell all but the boldest flavors. You can add prunes with tasty results. Apricots, too, do well, and then there are fresh dates. Try figs, too. They have to be added almost at the last minute, but are worth it. I've also included a tasty banana bread (Kickapoo Joy Bread).

Leftovers, or the Miscellaneous File: "Refrigerator gleanings" is good. "Waste not, want not." I mean those wonderful, nutritious scraps of things that you otherwise would leave in the refrigerator until they're beyond rescue. They can include: French toast mix, potatoes, oatmeal, cream of wheat or polenta, apple sauce, pancake mix, small amounts of cheese dip or sauce, or dried-up cheese, always an excellent thing. Regardless of how hard it has become, you can always grate it. I figure it as part of the shortening. My wife once used some leftover ham and pineapple. Leftover sausage is good. Some spaghetti sauce can make an excellent contribution to an interesting variation barchetta. If you are hesitant about adding lumpy but nutritious table scraps to your bread, don't worry. Just make a basic bread dough on the dough cycle. When it is ready, roll it out and put some of those various lumpy leftovers on the dough, roll it up, and bake it. How do you think the first pizza came about or, for that matter, stromboli?

Sourdough Starter: You can use a sourdough starter in your bread maker. It is basically a mixture of equal parts flour and water, plus a little yeast, set out to sour in your fridge for a day or two. You have to use some yeast in with the starter. It is mainly for flavor, anyway. You can use other things to help sourdough: beer, lime juice, rye flour, etc. See page 121 for how to make your own sourdough starter. If you really want a good sour flavor, but you don't want to use a starter, start the dough the night before and just leave it in the bread machine until the next day when you need it. (Don't put any eggs in, however, as they could spoil.) Then prepare it. Even better, simply start the dough a couple of days before and let it sour in the fridge.

Vegetables: It seems, looking at the various commercial breads and bread mixes, the sine qua non of all Italinate fancy breads must contain sun-dried tomatoes and, of course, basil. Sun-dried tomatoes can get a bit pricey, and if it isn't summer what are you going to do? I've noticed plum tomatoes showing up on vegetable stands a lot of late. Take a half-dozen plum tomatoes, cut them in half lengthwise, set them on a paper plate, cover with wax paper, and put them in your microwave, set on half power (50%), and heat them for about 20 minutes or so to dry them.

Toasted Bread Crumbs: This is an old trick you might try to enhance the flavor and darken your rye or pumpernickel bread. Try taking ¼ cup of bread crumbs. Spread them on a cookie sheet. Put them under your broiler for a few minutes — try 3 or 4 minutes — until dark brown. Measure bread crumbs in with the rye or pumpernickel flour in the bread recipe.

Spices

The Portuguese have a saying: *Port is the brother of cheese.* There are some spices to which this fine axiom also applies. If these spices aren't really brothers to bread, they are certainly shirttail kin. Here is a list of spices that you should have for use in bread. While not all of them are called for in the recipes, for variety's sake they can be used in many of them. Keep in mind that flour absorbs flavors, so usually you can safely add a greater quantity of most of the spices I suggest.

Allspice: It is called allspice because it tastes like cinnamon, clove, nutmeg, and juniper berry. I use it instead of the ones below when I just want a generic spicy flavor.

Cardamom: This had been a more popular spice at one time. If I have anything to do with it, it will be again. It doesn't taste quite like any other spice. It is an Indian spice, best when bought as the whole seed or pod, and ground as needed. It works particularly well in sweet doughs.

Cinnamon: First of the old standbys. Great, if not necessary, in raisin bread, and what would cinnamon rolls be without it? Small amounts remain initially undetected, save that the flavor is enhanced a bit.

Cloves: Use carefully. Cloves tend to take over whatever they are in, but in sweet dough (for breads and rolls), a little goes a long way in enhancing the flavor. Put a little — ¼ teaspoon of ground cloves, at most — in with your raisin bread or cinnamon rolls.

Ginger: I included a recipe for gingerbread that uses fresh ginger, now readily available at grocery stores. It is a staple in the cooking of the Orient and a wonderful treat in the dough recipes of the West. It is easier to use it ground in sweet or savory doughs. Candied ginger is one of the world's great treats, finely minced and added to sweet doughs or biscuits. Mix it with allspice, and you have pretty well covered the flavor spectrum.

Mace is nutmeg, only a little more. It is the outer part of the actual nut of the nutmeg. Some cooks put it in almost anything. My father-in-law, a chef for fifty years, says, "Put it in instant potatoes. It makes them taste real." (I'm not sure of that.)

Nutmeg: The real advantage of nutmeg over mace is that it is usually available and easily used, freshly ground. It does nice things to all breads, believe it or not. Good in potato breads with turmeric.

Turmeric: Use only a little, about ¼ teaspoon to 3 cups flour. It colors the dough a nice yellow, and adds something like a base to the flavor.

Saffron: Try it in some of the doughs with egg. Challah, for instance, benefits from the gentle, slightly bitter flavor of saffron, not to mention the color. No more than ¼ teaspoon, if that. Soak it in boiling water for 15 minutes; then add to the liquid ingredients in the dough mix.

Sesame and Poppy Seeds: Just delightful toppings for breads, both oven-baked and machine-baked. The sesame seeds add a hint of nuttiness; the poppy seeds add that nice flavor. If you use them as topping on loaves baked in your machine, do this: Before the dough begins to bake, open the lid and spray the dough with water; then sprinkle the seeds on it.

Bread Machine Mixes:
Prepare Your Own and Save Money

Let's say you know nothing whatsoever about making bread, and you just got a bread machine. Further, let's say it came without an instruction booklet. How would you make a loaf of bread in it? Well, you could buy a package of bread machine mix. Or you could take the following ingredients:

1 C warm water (cost, 2 cents)

3 C flour (cost, 25 cents)

1½ tsp of salt (cost, 1 cent)

1 of those expensive packages of yeast (cost, 35 cents)

You put all of these things, in the order listed above, into your bread machine, press the start button, and in a few hours you should have a nice, tasty, nutritious loaf of bread. This delicious loaf of bread should cost you less than $1.00 (about 15 shillings in the UK). In other words, it's cheap.

So if bread is essentially made up of just water, flour, salt, and yeast, you can see why I tend to regard store-bought bread machine mixes as an absurd thing on which to spend your hard-earned money. Admittedly, some of the more expensive packages of bread machine mix have some interesting ingredients, to wit: sun-dried tomatoes, basil, shallots, dill, and for the sweeter loaves, cinnamon and raisins. But what is there in any of them that you can't easily get yourself, and more cheaply?

But, suppose you come home tired, or at the last minute it dawns on you that you have no bread, and you've run out of flour, wouldn't it be nice to just dump a bag into the bread machine, add some water, and/or whatever, press the start button, and in a few hours have your little machine reward you with a nice loaf of bread? For the sake of those moments I present to you below, at substantial savings and at least comparable quality to commercial mixes, your own bread machine mixes.

How to Make a Bread Machine Mix
This seems like a leisure-time activity, to be done on a quiet Saturday or Sunday afternoon, while watching a game or maybe a movie.

First off, you'll need something in which to keep the mix. Those handy, quart-size, self-sealing plastic bags are just the thing; you probably already have them around. You'll need some kind of container to mix the mix in and to ease the pouring of said mix into the bag. A 4-cup measuring cup would be convenient. How about something to hold the bag upright and open? You'll need measuring spoons and a wooden spoon or spatula, for stirring. Some stick-on notes or labels or adhesive labels to jot some instructions on would be a good thing. **Note:** Once the mixes are prepared, you'll need to store them in a cool, dry, dark place.

Clear yourself some counter space, and line up your salt, sugar, and other ingredients. We'll start with a most typical mix and give it a name such as you might expect if you were shelling out a lot of money for it.

Deluxe Super Nutritious, Master Baker's Scrumptious White Bread

With the mixing container holding the open storage bag, measure into it:

>2 C bread flour or all-purpose flour*

>2 T dried milk solids

>2 T soy flour

>1 T gluten*

>½ tsp salt

>1 T sugar

*If you're using bread flour, omit the gluten.

Stir all of this with the spoon or spatula. Then add another:

>1 C flour.

Write the following on the label: "Put into the bread pan of the bread machine 1 cup water (or ½ cup milk and ½ cup water), 1 tablespoon shortening (lard, butter, margarine), then the bread mix, 1½ tsp yeast, and start." The half water/half milk combination is delicious. You can use all milk for an incredibly super deluxe, rich, chewy, soft-crusted loaf. Just plain water will yield a better loaf than the white bread you buy in stores. The yield should be a 1½ lb loaf of good bread.

Yummy Acres Farm-Fresh Blue-Ribbon-Winning Bread

Assemble your ingredients. With the mixing container holding the open storage bag, measure the following into the bag:

1 C bread flour or all-purpose flour*

1 C whole wheat flour

2 T dried milk solids

1 T gluten*

1 T wheat germ (or 2 tsp graham flour)

1½ tsp salt

2 T brown sugar**

*If you're using bread flour, omit the gluten.
**Or leave out the brown sugar and note that you must add 2 T of honey on the label.

Give the above a little stir with the wooden spoon; then add another:

1 C white flour.

On the label write the following: "Put into the bread pan of the bread maker 1 C apple cider or orange juice (or ½ C milk and ½ C water), 1½ T shortening (lard, butter, margarine), then the bread mix, 2 tsp yeast, and start." You should be able to plow about 20 acres after a couple of slices of this bread.

Old World Savory Euro Rye

How about this, for tasty sandwiches? Assemble your ingredients.
With the mixing container holding the open storage bag, measure the following into the bag:

> 1½ C bread or all-purpose flour*
>
> ½ C coarse-ground rye flour
>
> 1 T wheat germ (or 2 T graham flour)
>
> 2 T gluten*
>
> 1½ tsp salt
>
> 1½ T brown sugar**

*If you use bread flour, omit the gluten.
**Or leave out the brown sugar and note that you must add 1½ T honey on the label.

Give the above a little stir with the wooden spoon; then add another:

> 1 C flour.

On the label, write the following: "Put into the bread pan of the bread maker 1 C water, 1½ T shortening (olive oil or lard), then the bread mix, 2 tsp yeast, and start."

Euro-Taste Dinner Bread

You can make this loaf on the dough setting and use it as a pizza crust; you can make all of the breads on the dough setting, for that matter. Assemble your ingredients. With the mixing container holding the open storage bag, measure the following into the bag:

> 2 C bread or all-purpose flour*
>
> ¼ C coarse-ground rye flour
>
> 1 T gluten*
>
> 1½ tsp salt
>
> 1 tsp to 1 T basil (fresh or dried) or 1 T Italian seasoning
>
> 1½ T brown sugar**

*If you use bread flour, omit the gluten.
**Or leave out the brown sugar and note on the label that you must add 1½ T honey.

Give the above a little stir with the wooden spoon, then add another:

> 1 C flour.

On the label write the following: "Put into the bread pan of the bread maker 1 C water, 2 T olive oil, the bread mix; then add 2 tsp yeast, and start. Either 5 minutes before the last kneading, or when your beeper tells you, add 6 halves of sun-dried tomatoes and between 1 and 2 T parmesan cheese. You should be able to do an aria or two from *Rigoletto* after this.

Rich, Sweet Farm-Fresh North American Raisin Bread

Assemble your ingredients. With the mixing container holding the open storage bag, measure the following into the bag:

1 C bread flour or all-purpose flour*

1 C whole wheat flour

1 T dried milk solids

1 T gluten*

1½ tsp salt

1 tsp cinnamon

½ tsp each ginger and mace (or nutmeg)

2 T brown sugar**

*If you use bread flour, omit the gluten.
** Or leave out the brown sugar and note to add 2 T honey on the label.

Give the above a little stir with the wooden spoon; then add another:

1 C flour.

In a separate small bag or plastic wrap, wrap tightly: ⅓ C raisins and ⅓ C nuts (pecans, almonds, or peanuts).

On the label, write the following: "Put into the bread pan of the bread maker 1 C apple cider or orange juice (or ½ C milk and ½ C water), 1½ T shortening (lard, butter, margarine). Then add the mix, add 2 tsp yeast, and start. Near the last 5 minutes of the last kneading, or 15 to 20 minutes into the cycle (if you haven't a guide book or can't figure out when the last 5 minutes are), drop in ⅓ C raisins and ⅓ C nuts."

Grandmother Stoltzfuse's Old-Fashioned Central Pennsylvania Potato White Bread

Assemble your ingredients. With the mixing container holding the open storage bag, measure the following into the bag:

2 C bread or all-purpose flour*

2 T dried milk solids

2 T instant potato flakes

¼ tsp ground nutmeg

¼ tsp ground turmeric (optional)**

1 T gluten*

1½ tsp salt

1 T sugar

Stir all the above with a spoon or spatula; then add another:

1 C flour.

*If you're using bread flour, omit the gluten.
**In central Pennsylvania, this is often used to color the bread and leave a hint of the turmeric flavor.

Write the following on the label: "Put into the bread pan of the bread machine 1 C water, 1 T shortening (lard, butter, margarine), then the bread mix; add 1½ tsp yeast, and start." **Note:** If you have some, potato water would go nicely in this, instead of water.

Some History and Very Basic Bread Recipes

There is always that one bread recipe, that prime or basic recipe, the most ancient one, the genesis of them all. That simple combination of flour and water (in a ratio of 3 flour to 1 water), plus salt and yeast. Here it is:

> 1 C water
>
> 3 C flour
>
> 1½ tsp salt
>
> 1 tsp yeast

Combine these 4 ingredients, in the order given above, in the pan of your bread machine, and press the start button. You remove the bread when done. And people almost cheer, they wonder what it is, what magic you've worked. The smell of it, the taste and texture — Bread! I love it!

When I gave the above recipe to a supervisor at one of the major bread machine manufacturers, her first comment was: "Can you do that?"

"Of course you can," said I. And why would you? Well, because it's good.

After several thousand years it is still, you'll have to admit, just about the best. The only thing wrong with the above is that it doesn't last. (This may not even be anything wrong, per se, but in the very nature of it. To call it "wrong" would be like saying fresh flowers aren't any good, since they wilt and die.) Within a few hours, this bread is already becoming stale, and by the next day it is fit only for something generally regarded as French toast (which the French themselves call, when they call it at all, *pain perdu*).

Anyway, that basic bread recipe seems to have had its start in the Mediterranean area, primarily Egypt, but variations of it show up in other areas of the world, some with perhaps an even older tradition of bread baking — among the ancient Swiss lake dwellers of approximately 10 000 years ago, for instance. They had a serious baking industry. Imagine people baking bread 10 000 years ago — without a bread machine. As recently as ancient Rome, a mere 2000 years ago, there were over 250 bakeries in the Eternal City. What were the flours used? Good old wheat, of course, from Egypt. Egypt was Rome's bread basket. The predominant grain used in bread making over the centuries has been wheat. But rye was used, and probably barley and millet.

Now back to that first recipe: add oil or other shortening, which helps retain moisture, and the product begins to change and stays soft and fresh, or lasts longer. Adding sweetening to the bread dough also helps retain moisture and resist aging. But the more things are added, the more the basic rich wheaty taste is obscured, and the next thing you know, you are at the next basic recipe, the one with which most Americans are familiar, and on which most have grown up. It is the recipe I think of as fancy, or royalty bread.

I'm sure you're aware that white bread originally was for the well-to-do, royalty and such. The dark breads (the whole-grain breads, those hearty breads with the cheap, coarse meals and grains) were for the rest of us. Things, of course, change. Now the well-to-do, the new royalty, and such, favor those wholesome, rich, dark breads which give life and energy to those who work out for living.

What you add to the recipes, in what quantity, quality, variation, et cetera, determines what the bread is going to be like when you're through baking it. When you experiment with your own creations, the fun part is finding a name for them, and eating them, of course.

Here are some very basic bread recipes. From these several basics, all the various and sundry bread recipes are made, including the ones you can make up yourself. In illustrating these recipes, I am using the proportions for the 1½ lb loaf of bread. You can maintain the same ratio and enlarge, double, triple, etc.

Good Old #1

Ancient or first bread as we know and love it.

> 1 C warm water
>
> 3 C flour
>
> 1½ tsp salt
>
> 1 tsp yeast

Good Old #2

Probably more ancient and just as reliable.

1 C warm water	3 C whole wheat flour
2 T oil	1 T honey
1½ tsp salt	1½ tsp yeast

Good Old #3

1 C warm water	2 C flour
1 C rye flour	1½ tsp salt
2 tsp yeast	

#4: The First Attempt to Get Fancy

1 egg + water to make 1C	3 C flour
1 T sugar	1½ tsp salt
1½ tsp yeast	

#5: The First Fancy or Royalty Bread

½ C water	½ C milk
3 C flour	1 T shortening
1 T sugar	1½ tsp salt
1½ tsp yeast	

#6: The First Royal Crowd-Pleaser Bread

½ C water   ½ C milk

3 C flour   1 T shortening

2 T honey   1½ tsp salt

2 tsp yeast

After mixing the above, add generous portions of fruit and nuts.

Choosing a Recipe

Selecting the type of bread you are going to bake can be, and should be, though it rarely is, determined by that with which you intend to eat it, when you are going to eat it, and even (strange as this may seem) what time of year it is.

You may not want to have a rich, milk-and-butter laden slice of bread on a hot summer morning. On a hot summer morning, a light, slightly sweet version of a baguette is in order, perhaps with a bit of ginger or citrus butter spread upon it. On a cold fall or winter morning, when you know you are going to be out and about, you load up on the carbs, with something like my Parker House Loaf (page 42) — nothing like it for when you are going to rake leaves, shovel snow, pummel the grandchildren with snowballs, or maybe even just take a brisk constitutional.

The same with luncheons. If you work for a living, a good roast beef or Black Forest ham sandwich demands a rich whole wheat or rye platform on which to stack it. For dinner? If you are having one of those summer Greek style, assemble-your-own dinners, the ancient Mediterranean, lightly salted, shortening-free loaves, baked a half-hour before, are absolutely essential. They're especially good sliced lengthwise, coated with olive oil, and spread with fresh-squeezed garlic.

Your breads should go with your meals, just as your wine or beer does. And that means your breads can and should be just as varied — mated, as it were — with the food on your table.

Some Useful Recipe Tips

The recipes in the preceding section were an attempt to show the development and similarities of all bread recipes. Now come the real thing, provided for the three common sizes of bread machines. The column headings indicate the size of the bread maker for which the ingredients are designed. You can make the 1 and the 1½ lb size bread recipes in the 2-lb machine also, so if the 2-lb recipe produces more bread than you need, you can make a smaller size recipe next time.

A Reminder Concerning Yeast: All the recipes in this book are based on using rapid-rise, or quick-rise, or instant yeast. If you are using regular dried yeast, you will have to add a bit more yeast, perhaps as much as ½ teaspoon more, to the recipe.

Here are some guidelines for using the recipes that follow:

1. The basic labor part of all these recipes is the same. You measure all the ingredients, in the order they are given. (I specify putting in the liquid first. If your bread machine specifies putting the dry ingredients in first, do that.) Select the appropriate time or cycle, and start the operation.

2. All of the recipes that follow can be made equally well on the dough cycle, and probably better, rather than being baked in the machine. Just remove the dough from the machine when it has risen, then knead the loaf for a minute or two to make sure all the air is out. Then select the bread pan of your choice, place the dough in it, and let it rise again to at least double in bulk. You can make it round, or like a log (a baguette) or even in two small loaves. You get the picture.

3. Remember that we are dealing with natural ingredients — water, flour, salt, etc. Try as manufacturers might, things such as flour are never always the same; wet years and dry, flour from Canada or Texas — the variables are almost infinite. Also, your water is not going to be the same as my water, and so forth. Our various baking practices must adapt to the existential situation we find.

4. Test the dough. Fortunately, things are not all that different among recipes. So, when you are making a recipe for the first time, after the ingredients have been in the machine for 5 minutes or so and have actually become dough, open the machine and touch the dough ball (be careful; you don't want to catch your finger in the kneading paddle). If the dough seems

wet and sticky or looks gooey, add more flour. Do this in approximate tablespoons. Add one, give the machine a moment to absorb the flour, then another, until the dough is right: soft to the touch, but only slightly sticky.

If, on the other hand, the dough seems dry or it starts to lump up, and if the bread machine sounds like it's having trouble kneading the dough, add a little water; again, a tablespoon at a time. You'll hear the machine start working better almost immediately. You'll get the hang of all this quickly and soon develop baker's instinct. When that kicks in, you'll just know how much flour, or water, will make it right.

5. Don't feel that you have to follow these recipes exactly. Use your common sense. What if the recipe calls for say, 4 cups of flour, and you discover at the last minute you only have about 3½? Take out an ounce or two of water! If it calls for 2 tablespoons of margarine and you have less than one, add a bit of butter or oil to make up the difference. If the recipe calls for honey, and you're out, sugar or molasses, or even brown sugar, can be substituted. For liquids, if you find some leftover apple juice, or any kind of juice in the bottom of the fridge, toss it in with the water. For the most part substitutions in bread will at the most change the bread only a little. The important thing is not to be intimidated. Keep the basic wet–dry proportions in mind, don't forget the yeast and salt, and almost anything that comes out of your bread machine is going to be pretty good. This goes for almost any ingredient except yeast or salt. If you find you are short a teaspoon of yeast, then you better go get some; the same with salt.

6. About flour: For the most part I use only the term "flour" in the recipes. The stronger or more potent bread flour, or professional flour, gives you a better loaf of bread, but if you have only good old-fashioned all-purpose white flour, use it. You're still going to get a good loaf of bread. Remember that I suggested you buy some gluten? Use some of that gluten when you are using all-purpose flour. If you don't have the gluten, you're still going to get a pretty good loaf of bread. You can try adding a bit (like ¼ teaspoon) more yeast and another teaspoon of sugar. There are one or two recipes where I specify all-purpose flour (dinner rolls or sweet breads, that kind of thing; you want them to be a little softer). If all you have is bread flour, you can use it; they'll just have a bit more crust.

Basic Breads

Just Plain Bread

Let us begin with the basic bread and the variations thereof. Here it is, again, good old #1. But here let's call it Just Plain Bread.

1 lb	1½ lb	2 lb
1 C water	1¼ C water	1½ C water
2½ C flour	3¼ C flour	4 C flour
1½ tsp salt	2 tsp salt	2½ tsp salt
1 tsp yeast	1½ tsp yeast	2 tsp yeast

Load the ingredients into your bread pan. This loaf works in the rapid or quick-bake cycle, but because of the lack of extra sugar to feed the yeast, it really needs more time, so it is best done on the regular cycle, or even the French bread cycle (I've even seen it called European loaf cycle).

Mediterranean Style Just Plain Bread

1 lb	1½ lb	2 lb
⅞ C water	1⅛ C water	1½ C water
2½ C flour	3½ C flour	4½ C flour
1 T rye flour	1½ T rye flour	2 T rye flour
2 T olive oil*	3 T olive oil*	4 T olive oil*
1½ tsp salt	2 tsp salt	2½ tsp salt
1 tsp yeast	1½ tsp yeast	2 tsp yeast

*For an even softer, maybe tastier loaf, substitute lard for the olive oil.

Peasant Bread

I'm not sure this is what peasants eat. There may not even be any peasants left. If not, we can always call it a rustic loaf. Anyway, I've had some good Italian breads in New York that I will bet use the following ingredients.

1 lb	1½ lb	2 lb
⅞ C water	1⅛ C water	1½ C water
2½ C flour	4 C flour	5 C flour
1 T whole wheat flour	1½ T whole wheat flour	2 T whole wheat flour
2 T olive oil	3 T olive oil	4 T olive oil
1 T honey	1½ T honey	2 T honey
1½ tsp salt	2 tsp salt	2½ tsp salt
1 tsp yeast	1½ tsp yeast	2 tsp yeast

Summer Bread

I call this Summer Bread because, unlike thick, dense loaves with lots of fat, this one is light and rather airy. It is ideal if your machine has one of those Euro or French settings. It really is best when made with either bread flour or high-gluten flour. You can even substitute ¼ C semolina for ¼ C of the flour measurement.

1 lb	1½ lb	2 lb
⅞ C water	1⅛ C water	1½ C water
2½ C bread flour*	3½ C bread flour*	5 C bread flour*
1 T gluten*	1½ T gluten*	2 T gluten*
1 tsp olive oil	2 tsp olive oil	1 T olive oil
½ tsp lemon juice	1 tsp lemon juice	1½ tsp lemon juice
1 tsp sugar	1½ tsp sugar	2 tsp sugar
1 tsp salt	1½ tsp salt	2 tsp salt
1 tsp yeast	1½ tsp yeast	2 tsp yeast

If you're not using bread flour or high-gluten flour, add the gluten.

Northern Euro Bread

I can't say for a fact that the northern European breads are made like this, but I can say they taste like this. I've noted, anyway, that the farther north you go, as reflected in European breads, the more saturated fats are used: lards, butter, milk. The colder it gets, the more you need fat. The consequence of adding fat is that the loaves last longer, have softer textures, and make great toast.

1 lb	1½ lb	2 lb
⅞ C water	1⅛ C water	1½ C water
2¼ C flour	3¼ C flour	4 C flour
2 T rye flour	2½ T rye flour	3 T rye flour
1 T lard	1½ T lard	2 T lard
2 tsp honey	1 T honey	1½ T honey
1½ tsp salt	2 tsp salt	2½ tsp salt
1 tsp yeast	1½ tsp yeast	2 tsp yeast

Rich, Dark Mediterranean Style Bread

1 lb	1½ lb	2 lb
1 C water	1¼ C water	1½ C water
1½ C flour	2 C flour	3¼ C flour
1 C whole wheat flour	1⅓ C whole wheat flour	1½ C whole wheat flour
1 T rye flour	1½ T rye flour	2 T rye flour
2 T oil*	3 T oil*	4 T oil*
1½ tsp salt	2 tsp salt	2½ tsp salt
1 tsp yeast	1½ tsp yeast	2 tsp yeast

*For an even softer, maybe tastier loaf, substitute lard for the oil.

Bread with Savory Stuff in It

I had thought about a whole section on "stuff" (things you add to the dough) in this book. But, as I've said repeatedly, almost anything edible can go into bread, so what I decided to do was to have basic recipes — sweet and savory — keep the recipes simple, and make suggestions on what kind of stuff to put in. You'll note the mention of gluten again. Because stuff has a tendency to inhibit the rising of dough, a little strengthening of the dough is a good idea. If you're using bread flour, you can skip the gluten. The dough with sweet goodies is on page 48. Here is the recipe for the savory version.

1 lb	1½ lb	2 lb
⅞ C water	1¼ C water	1½ C water
2½ C flour*	4 C flour*	5 C flour*
1 T gluten*	1½ T gluten*	2 T gluten*
1 T rye flour	1½ T rye flour	2 T rye flour
2 T olive oil**	3 T olive oil**	4 T olive oil**
1½ tsp salt	2 tsp salt	2½ tsp salt
1½ tsp yeast	2 tsp yeast	2½ tsp yeast

5 minutes before the end of mixing, add:

⅓ C stuff	⅓ C stuff	⅓ C stuff

*If you're using bread flour or high-gluten flour, omit the gluten.
**For an even softer, maybe tastier loaf, substitute lard for the oil.

At the last 5 minutes of kneading, or at the "stuff" beeper: add pieces of dried tomatoes with dried onions and some leftover pepperoni. Or grate some dried cheese, add some leftover sausage or hamburger or ham (my wife threw some ham and pineapple in once). Chopped peanuts are good, as are pine nuts if you have them around. Try a tablespoon of some Old Bay Seasoning, or salad dressing, those curious bacon-flavored bits, or the real thing — even better.

Very Basic Whole Wheat Bread

1 lb	1½ lb	2 lb
1 C water	1⅛ C water	1½ C water
2¼ C flour	2¾ C flour	3½ C flour
½ C whole wheat flour	¾ C whole wheat flour	1 C whole wheat flour
1 T oil	1½ T oil	2 T oil
1 T butter	1½ T butter	2 T butter
1 T honey	1½ T honey	2 T honey
1½ tsp salt	2 tsp salt	2½ tsp salt
1 tsp yeast	1½ tsp yeast	2 tsp yeast

Three Good Rye Breads

Interesting Light Rye Bread

1 lb	1½ lb	2 lb
1 C water	1¼ C water	1½ C water
2 C flour	2½ C flour	3 C flour
1 T gluten*	1½ T gluten*	2 T gluten*
1 C rye flour	1½ C rye flour	2 C rye flour
2 T olive oil**	3 T olive oil**	4 T olive oil**
1½ tsp salt	2 tsp salt	2½ tsp salt
1½ tsp yeast	2 tsp yeast	2½ tsp yeast
Options:		
½ tsp dill weed	¾ tsp dill weed	1 tsp dill weed
1 tsp caraway seed	1½ tsp caraway seed	2 tsp caraway seed
1 tsp fennel seed	1½ tsp fennel seed	2 tsp fennel seed

*If you are not using bread flour or high-gluten flour, I suggest you add gluten to the flour.
**For an even softer, maybe tastier loaf, substitute lard for the olive oil.

There are three options for you to try, all together or one at a time, to spice up your bread.

Interesting Dark Rye Bread

Try the options, together or one at a time, for added flavor.

1 lb	1½ lb	2 lb
1 C water	1¼ C water	1½ C water
2 C flour	2½ C flour	3 C flour
1 T gluten*	1½ T gluten*	2 T gluten*
1 C rye flour	1½ C rye flour	2 C rye flour
1 tsp instant coffee	1½ tsp instant coffee	2 tsp instant coffee
2 T olive oil**	3 T olive oil**	4 T olive oil**
1½ tsp salt	2 tsp salt	2½ tsp salt
2 tsp brown sugar	3 tsp brown sugar	4 tsp brown sugar
1½ tsp yeast	2 tsp yeast	2¼ tsp yeast
Options:		
½ tsp dill weed	¾ tsp dill weed	1 tsp dill weed
1 tsp caraway seeds	1½ tsp caraway seeds	2 tsp caraway seeds
1 tsp fennel seeds	1½ tsp fennel seeds	2 tsp fennel seeds

*If you are not using bread flour or high-gluten flour, I suggest you add gluten.
**For an even softer, maybe tastier loaf, substitute lard for the olive oil.

Even More Interesting Dark Rye Bread

1 lb	1½ lb	2 lb
1 C water	1¼ C water	1½ C water
1 tsp instant coffee	1½ tsp instant coffee	2 tsp instant coffee
2 tsp molasses	3 tsp molasses	1 T molasses
1 C flour*	1½ C flour*	2 C flour*
1 T gluten*	1½ T gluten*	2 T gluten*
¾ C whole wheat flour	1 C whole wheat flour	1½ C whole wheat flour
¾ C rye flour	1 C rye flour	1½ C rye flour
1 tsp cocoa	1½ tsp cocoa	2 tsp cocoa
2 T margarine	3 T margarine	4 T margarine
1 tsp caraway seeds	1½ tsp caraway seeds	2 tsp caraway seeds
1½ tsp salt	2 tsp salt	2½ tsp salt
1½ tsp yeast	2 tsp yeast	2½ tsp yeast

*If you are not using bread flour or high-gluten flour, I suggest you add gluten to the flour.

The Fancy Breads

Note: In this section of the book, where we are combining different liquids, I sometimes give the liquid measurement in ounces. I find they are a little easier to read than fractions such as ⅞ or ⅝. But when they are simple, I mean really simple, I revert; ¼ cup, for instance is easier than 2 ounces.

Basic Good Old North American Bread

1 lb	1½ lb	2 lb
5 oz water	7 oz water	1 C water
2 oz milk	3 oz milk	½ C milk
3 C flour	4 C flour	5 C flour
1 T sugar	1½ T sugar	2 T sugar
1 tsp lemon juice	1½ tsp lemon juice	2 tsp lemon juice
1 T lard*	1½ T lard*	2 T lard*
1½ tsp salt	2 tsp salt	2½ tsp salt
1¼ tsp yeast	1½ tsp yeast	2 tsp yeast

*Or other shortening.

Richer Still North American or Kids' Bread

1 lb	1½ lb	2 lb
⅞ C (water + milk)*	1⅛ C (water + milk)*	1½ C (water + milk)*
2½ C flour	3½ C flour	5 C flour
1½ T sugar	2 T sugar	2½ T sugar
1 tsp lemon juice	1½ tsp lemon juice	2 tsp lemon juice
1 T lard	1½ T lard	2 T lard
1½ tsp salt	2 tsp salt	2½ tsp salt
1¼ tsp yeast	1½ tsp yeast	2 tsp yeast

*The mixture should be half water/half milk.

Really Fancy Bread

1 lb	1½ lb	2 lb
7 oz milk	1⅛ C milk	1½ C milk
2½ C flour	3½ C flour	5 C flour
1½ T sugar	2 T sugar	2½ T sugar
1 tsp lemon juice	1½ tsp lemon juice	2 tsp lemon juice
1 T butter	1½ T butter	2 T butter
1½ tsp salt	2 tsp salt	2½ tsp salt
1 tsp yeast	1½ tsp yeast	2 tsp yeast

Big Kids' Whole Wheat Bread

1 lb	1½ lb	2 lb
½ C water	⅝ C water	¾ C water
½ C milk	⅝ C milk	¾ C milk
2 C flour	2½ C flour	3 C flour
1 C whole wheat flour	1½ C whole wheat flour	2 C whole wheat flour
2 T honey	2½ T honey	3 T honey
1 T butter	1½ T butter	2 T butter
1½ tsp salt	2 tsp salt	2½ tsp salt
1½ tsp yeast	1¾ tsp yeast	2 tsp yeast

Parker House Loaf

Here is another good Sunday morning special. The name comes from its flavor. It is slightly different from the Parker House dough recipe. It stays fresh well, so you can have it as toast, yes, even French toast, on Monday (if there is any of it left after Sunday). You'll love it.

1 lb	1½ lb	2 lb
1 egg & (water + milk) to ⅞ C total*	1 egg & (water + milk) to 1⅛ C total*	1 egg & (water + milk) to 1½ C total*
2½ C flour	3½ C flour	5 C flour
1½ T sugar	2 T sugar	2½ T sugar
1 tsp lemon juice	1½ tsp lemon juice	2 tsp lemon juice
1 T margarine	1½ T margarine	2 T margarine
⅛ tsp saffron or turmeric**	¼ tsp saffron or turmeric**	⅓ tsp saffron or turmeric**
1½ tsp salt	2 tsp salt	2½ tsp salt
1½ tsp yeast	1¾ tsp yeast	2 tsp yeast

*The mixture should be half milk, half water. See my comments on egg measurement in the ingredients section (pg 16).
**See spice section for using saffron or turmeric.

Raisin-Nut Whole Wheat Bread

Here's another breakfast bread. The first ingredient is juice: apple, cranberry, grape, or orange. The original recipe from which I adapted this
called for walnuts. I like pecans; if you have neither, try peanuts, or even
cashews. Don't skip this tasty loaf over a little thing like nuts. If you have
some walnut oil, here's where you use it.

1 lb	1½ lb	2 lb
⅔ C juice	¾ C juice	1 C juice
⅓ C yogurt	½ C yogurt	½ C yogurt
2 C flour	2½ C flour	3 C flour
1 C whole wheat flour	1½ C whole wheat flour	2 C whole wheat flour
2 T honey	2½ T honey	3 T honey
1 T margarine or oil	1½ T margarine or oil	2 T margarine or oil
1½ tsp salt	2 tsp salt	2½ tsp salt
1½ tsp yeast	2 tsp yeast	2¼ tsp yeast

Add at the fruit beeper or 5 minutes before the end of mixing:

¼ C raisins	¼ C raisins	¼ C raisins
⅓ C chopped nuts	⅓ C chopped nuts	⅓ C chopped nuts

Hot Bread

Good with tame chili. A sandwich bread like you've never before tasted.

1 lb	1½ lb	2 lb
⅞ C water	1¼ C water	1½ C water
2¼ C flour	3 C flour	4 C flour
1 T rye flour	1½ T rye flour	2 T rye flour
1 T vinegar	1¼ T vinegar	1½ T vinegar
2 T olive oil*	3 T olive oil*	4 T olive oil*
¼ tsp garlic powder	¼+ tsp garlic powder	½ tsp garlic powder
½ tsp black pepper	¾ tsp black pepper	1 tsp black pepper
¼ tsp cayenne pepper	¼+ tsp cayenne pepper	½ tsp cayenne pepper
1½ tsp salt	2 tsp salt	2½ tsp salt
1¼ tsp yeast	1½ tsp yeast	2 tsp yeast

At the last 5 minutes of kneading, or at the "stuff" beeper, you could add drained green chilies and/or pieces of dried tomatoes and/or dried onions and some of those curious bacon-flavored bits, or — even better — the real thing.

Cornbread

Cornbread is an important part of any diet, especially one that includes chili. The question my wife asked was: "Can it be made easily in the bread machine, and at the same time come close to that wonderful traditional recipe, the baking-powder-leavened stuff?"

"Hmmmm," I opined, "Why not?"

In the American southland, I counted no less than 7 kinds of cornmeal, or corn flour: 3 each of white and yellow cornmeal, fine, medium, and coarse; plus corn flour, often called maize. In the northlands, we are used to seeing mainly good old yellow cornmeal (although in central Pennsylvania, I often see roasted cornmeal). The last time I was in the South, I stocked up. The following recipe was developed using fine white cornmeal. It's better with the traditional yellow cornmeal. Load and bake on regular cycle.

1 lb	1½ lb	2 lb
⅞ C buttermilk*	1 C buttermilk*	1⅛ C buttermilk*
1 egg beaten remove & discard 1 T	2 eggs, beaten remove & discard 2T	2 eggs
1½ C bread flour	2 C bread flour	3 C bread flour
1 T gluten**	1½ T gluten**	2 T gluten**
1 C cornmeal	1¼ C cornmeal	1¾ C cornmeal
½ tsp baking soda	¾ tsp baking soda	1 tsp baking soda
2 T sugar	2 T + 1 tsp sugar	3 T sugar
1 T shortening	1½ T shortening	2 T shortening
1 tsp salt	1½ tsp salt	2 tsp salt
1½ tsp yeast	2 tsp yeast	2½ tsp yeast*

*Trying to maintain the flavors of my preferred cornbread, I've stuck with buttermilk. If you want to use whole milk, skip the baking soda.
**If you are using all-purpose flour instead of bread flour, add the gluten.

Spicy Breakfast Bread

This bread does wonderful things for the fragrance of the whole house. The next day, it makes a French toast the likes of which you've never dreamed.

1 lb	1½ lb	2 lb
⅞ C orange juice	1⅛ C orange juice	1½ C orange juice
2¼ C flour	3 C flour	4 C flour
1½ T sugar	2 T sugar	2½ T sugar
1 tsp lemon juice	1½ tsp lemon juice	2 tsp lemon juice
1 T margarine	1½ T margarine	2 T margarine
1 tsp cinnamon	1½ tsp cinnamon	2 tsp cinnamon
½ tsp ginger	¾ tsp ginger	1 tsp ginger
¼ tsp nutmeg	½ tsp nutmeg	¾ tsp nutmeg
¼ tsp ground cloves	½ tsp ground cloves	¾ tsp ground cloves
1 tsp salt	1½ tsp salt	2 tsp salt
1¼ tsp yeast	1½ tsp yeast	2 tsp yeast

Potato White Bread

In the ingredients section, I mentioned saving potato cooking water. This is where you use it. I know there are recipes for Potato Bread that specify instant potatoes. We don't use instant potatoes; we use real potatoes, but you can get a similar effect by adding a tablespoon of dried potato flakes, if you have them around, and a tablespoon of water. This is a favorite bread at our house.

1 lb	1½ lb	2 lb
7 oz potato water	9 oz potato water	1⅓ C potato water
2⅓ C flour	3 C flour	4¼ C flour
1 T lard*	1½ T lard*	2 T lard*
1 T mashed potatoes	1½ T mashed potatoes	2 T mashed potatoes
1 T sugar	1½ T sugar	2 T sugar
1½ tsp salt	2 tsp salt	2½ tsp salt
1¼ tsp yeast	1½ tsp yeast	2 tsp yeast

*Use other shortening if you prefer.

There is a nice touch when making this bread. At the last rise, before the bread begins to bake in the bread machine, open the machine and toss in a generous teaspoon of flour. Traditionally, potato white bread is covered with flour, probably stemming from a time when the bread had actually risen by the action of potato water and tended to be a bit sticky. The farm ladies probably put extra flour on their hands to stop the dough from sticking, and so it was baked with the extra flour. You can help maintain that tradition.

Potato-Bacon Rye Bread

Here is still another use for potato water. But first off, chop up and then fry 4, 5, or 6 strips of bacon, depending upon the size recipe you are making. When the bacon is nice and crisp, remove and blot on paper towels. At this point you may want to chop some fresh onion and saute it in the bacon fat until transparent (about 2 or 3 minutes). Remove the onions and put them with the bacon. Then pour one (or 1½, or 2) tablespoons of the bacon fat into the bread pan. Add the potato water, then the rest of the ingredients. Add the chopped bacon pieces (and the onions if you use them) at the beep for the additions, or at about the last 5 minutes of the kneading cycle.

1 lb	1½ lb	2 lb
7 oz potato water	9 oz potato water	1 ⅓ C potato water
1½ C flour	2 C flour	3 C flour
¾ C rye flour	1 C rye flour	1½ C rye flour
1 T sugar	1½ T sugar	2 T sugar
1 T bacon fat*	1½ T bacon fat*	2 T bacon fat*
1½ tsp salt	2 tsp salt	2½ tsp salt
1½ tsp yeast	2 tsp yeast	2½ tsp yeast

Five minutes before the end of mixing, add:

chopped bacon pieces	chopped bacon pieces	chopped bacon pieces
chopped onions*	chopped onions*	chopped onions*

*Optional. Sauted fresh, or dried.

Bread with Sweet Stuff in It

Here is the basic recipe for adding sweet stuff in your bread. Sweet stuff means fruits and nuts, but not exclusively. You might try a handful of sweet breakfast cereal if there are a bunch of kids around. Because even sweet stuff has a tendency to inhibit the rising of dough, a little strengthening of the dough is a good idea, which is why you'll see the gluten.

1 lb	1½ lb	2 lb
⅞ C water	1¼ C water	1½ C water
2½ C flour	4 C flour	5 C flour
1 T gluten*	1½ T gluten*	2 T gluten*
2 T margarine	3 T margarine	4 T margarine
1 T sugar	1½ T sugar .	2 T sugar
1½ tsp salt	2 tsp salt	2½ tsp salt
1½ tsp yeast	2 tsp yeast	2½ tsp yeast

Five minutes before the end of mixing, add:

⅓ C stuff**	⅓ C stuff**	⅓ C stuff**

*If you're using bread flour, you can omit the gluten.
**Stuff can include: pieces of dried prunes, chopped dates, pineapple, grated dried cheese, leftover strawberries.... Chopped peanuts are good, as are pine nuts, if you have them around. Try a tablespoon of white wine or even sherry, but cut back on the other liquids proportionately. Add the stuff at the last 5 minutes of kneading, or at the "stuff" beeper.

Really Fancy Breads

Date-Nut Bread

You like date–nut bread? Try this really simple version. It is best when using really fresh dates, pitted and quartered. If the mixed nuts you are using are fairly large, chop them somewhat, about the same size as raisins. This bread is also best done on the Raisin Bread cycle. Otherwise, add the dates and nuts in the last 5 minutes of kneading.

1 lb	1½ lb	2 lb
½ C water	⅝ C water	¾ C water
½ C milk	⅝ C milk	¾ C milk
2 C flour	2½ C flour	3 C flour
1 C whole wheat flour	1½ C whole wheat flour	2 C whole wheat flour
1 T brown sugar	1½ T brown sugar	2 T brown sugar
1 T margarine	1½ T margarine	2 T margarine
1½ tsp salt	2 tsp salt	2½ tsp salt
1½ tsp yeast	2 tsp yeast	2½ tsp yeast

At the beeper, or 5 minutes before the end of mixing, add:

¼ C chopped dates	⅓ C chopped dates	½ C chopped dates
¼ C mixed nuts	⅓ C mixed nuts	½ C mixed nuts

Dried Cranberry Bread

Dried cranberries are expensive; one would think they would be a shade more flavorful. But good they are, nonetheless. The next question is: how to maximize the flavor potential of these little bits. It was my daughter Lydia who asked for the recipe. The first one isn't bad; not much to it, but then we're dealing with some highly flavorful stuff. The second one is really quite good.

Dried Cranberry Bread #1

1 lb loaf	1½ lb loaf	2 lb loaf
⅞ C cranberry juice	1⅛ C cranberry juice	1¼ C cranberry juice
2¼ C flour	3 C flour	4 C flour
1 tsp salt (scant)	1 tsp salt	1½ tsp salt
1 T sugar	1½ T sugar	2 T sugar
1 T shortening	1½ T shortening	2 T shortening
1¼ tsp yeast	1½ tsp yeast	2 tsp yeast

Five minutes before the end of mixing, add:

¼ C dried cranberries	⅓ C dried cranberries	½ C dried cranberries

Dried Cranberry Bread #2
(also called Cranorange Bread)

1 lb loaf	1½ lb loaf	2 lb loaf
¾ C orange juice	1⅛ C orange juice	1¼ C orange juice
1 T orange marmalade*	1½ T orange marmalade*	2 T orange marmalade*
2½ C flour	3¼ C flour	4 C flour
1 tsp salt (scant)	1 tsp salt	1½ tsp salt
2 tsp sugar	1 T sugar	1½ T sugar
½ T shortening	1 T shortening	1½ T shortening
1¼ tsp yeast	1½ tsp yeast	2 tsp yeast

Five minutes before the end of mixing, add:

¼ C dried cranberries	⅓ C dried cranberries	½ C dried cranberries

* Here's what you can do if you don't have any orange marmalade. Take the skin off a nice orange. Slice it very thin. Put this skin in a glass of water in which you've dissolved a teaspoon of sugar. Stick this it the microwave for 1½ minutes on high. Remove the orange peel, and use it instead of marmalade.

Gingerbread

As I woke up the other morning, this recipe came into my mind. Well, to tell the truth, the idea or, better yet, the name was in my mind. Gingerbread? How could you make a nice loaf of gingerbread in the bread machine? Could you make it either spicy and semi-sweet to have with bean soup, or hot and sweet to have as a breakfast loaf? So I went to my cookbooks and found several recipes, but none I could make in the bread machine. The first time I made it, I actually used fresh ginger, diced and sauteed in butter. I continued working on the recipes until I came up with the two here. They are really best if you use several pieces of candied ginger, minced, and then put them in the water you are going to use in the bread, heat them for one minute on high in the microwave, let them rest for 10 minutes, and then go ahead and make the bread. Try both recipes.

Spicy Gingerbread

This one is spicy and good for lunch or dinner.

1 lb loaf	1½ lb loaf	2 lb loaf
½ C water	⅔ C water	¾ C water
¼ C milk	⅓ C milk	½ C milk
¼ C molasses	⅓ C molasses	½ C molasses
2 C flour	2½ C flour	3 C flour
½ C whole wheat flour	¾ C whole wheat flour	1 C whole wheat flour
1 tsp salt (scant)	1½ tsp salt	2 tsp salt
1 T margarine	1½ T margarine	2 T margarine
1 tsp ginger	1¼ tsp ginger	1½ tsp ginger
½ tsp cinnamon	1 tsp cinnamon	1½ tsp cinnamon
¼ tsp ground cloves	⅓ tsp ground cloves	½ tsp ground cloves
1½ tsp yeast	2 tsp yeast	2½ tsp yeast

Sweet and Spicy Gingerbread

For breakfast. Of course there is going to be a question about the honey measurement. It is gooey and sticky. The way it is written could drive a recipe purist bananas. Which reminds me of that story about Alfred Hitchcock, when an actress was agonizing over her part. Hitchcock said: "For heaven's sake, it's only a movie." So I say: "For heaven's sake, it's only a loaf of bread." This is much better using crystallized or candied ginger.

1 lb loaf	1½ lb loaf	2 lb loaf
1 egg and water to total ¾ C*	1 egg and water to total 1 C*	1 egg and water to total 1⅛ C*
¼ C molasses	⅓ C molasses	½ C molasses
1 T honey	1 T (heaping) honey	2 T honey
2½ C flour	3 C flour	4 C flour
1 tsp salt (scant)	1½ tsp salt	2 tsp salt
1 T margarine	1½ T margarine	2 T margarine
1 tsp ginger	1¼ tsp ginger	1½ tsp ginger
½ tsp cinnamon	1 tsp cinnamon	1½ tsp cinnamon
¼ tsp ground cloves	⅓ tsp ground cloves	½ tsp ground cloves
1½ tsp yeast	2 tsp yeast	2¼ tsp yeast

*See my comments on egg measurement in the ingredients section (p. 16).

Fruit Cake Bread

Fruit cake is something of an acquired taste, at least it has been for me. Here is a loaf that bakes nicely in the bread machine. It hasn't the tutti frutti taste that most fruit cakes have. If you don't like fruit cakes, but kinda wish you did, try this. It is sweet, of course, and very rich, and the ginger transforms the whole thing. Chop the pecans to be about the size of raisins.

1 lb	1½ lb	2 lb
1 C water	1¼ C water	1½ C water
2 C flour	2½ C flour	3 C flour
½ C whole wheat flour	¾ C whole wheat flour	1 C whole wheat flour
2 T brown sugar	2½ T brown sugar	3 T brown sugar
1 T margarine	1½ T margarine	2 T margarine
1 tsp salt	1½ tsp salt	2 tsp salt
1½ tsp yeast	2 tsp yeast	2½ tsp yeast

At beeper or 5 minutes before end of mixing, add:

¼ C chopped dates	⅓ C chopped dates	½ C chopped dates
¼ C chopped pecans	⅓ C chopped pecans	½ C chopped pecans
¼ C chopped candied ginger	⅓ C chopped candied ginger	½ C chopped candied ginger

Trail Mix Bread

The first and obvious problem with this bread is the variety of trail mixes available. The solution is two types of trail mix bread, sweet and savory. Going on a hike? Pack this. First, the more savory of the two.

1 lb	1½ lb	2 lb
1 C water	1¼ C water	1½ C water
1½ C flour	2 C flour	2½ C flour
1 T gluten*	1½ T gluten*	2 T gluten*
1 C rye flour	1½ C rye flour	2 C rye flour
1 tsp brown sugar	1½ tsp brown sugar	2 tsp brown sugar
1 tsp salt	1½ tsp salt	2 tsp salt
1½ tsp yeast	2 tsp yeast	2½ tsp yeast

Add at beeper or 5 minutes before end of mixing:

¾ C trail mix	1 C trail mix	1¼ C trail mix
1 T olive oil**	2 T olive oil**	3 T olive oil**

*If you are not using bread flour or high-gluten flour, I suggest you add gluten to the flour.
**You'll need a good bit of fat if you're out there on the trail.

Use the raisin-bread setting, if your machine has one. Start the machine without the shortening (oil) or the trail mix, and run it 10 to 15 minutes (you're building up that gluten). Then, if your machine doesn't have an ingredients beeper, say on the raisin-bread cycle, do the following: Restart the machine, this time with the shortening; in the last 5 minutes of kneading, add the trail mix. These quantities of trail mix are arbitrary. Use more or less, as you choose, but remember the bread really should rise, and too much trail mix will inhibit the rising. For the sweeter version of the recipe, simply increase the sugar from teaspoon measurements to tablespoons.

Depending upon your packing requirements, you may want to do this loaf on the dough cycle; then shape it to fit the pan or your back pack. Or you can even do it rather like a really long baguette, and use it as an edible walking stick. Of course, you can sit out on the back porch, spread cheese on it, eat it with a tasty adult beverage, and read the great books. But then you'll have the problem about what to do with all the energy the bread gives.

Pandolce Genovese

Traditionally baked in a rather fancy pan. I've seen some like castles or churches, so the frequently odd shape of the bread machine pan works to advantage. I suggest removing the dough at the beginning of the last rise, before the baking phase; remove the kneading paddle and put some butter on the shaft. Knead the dough for perhaps a minute until all the air is out of it; then put back in the bread pan. When the loaf is finished and you remove it from the pan, you will notice the ¼-inch wide hole in the bottom of the loaf. If you want to, cut the top of the loaf to make it stand up straight, invert it, and stick a little Italian flag in the hole. This recipe cannot be made in the 1-lb machine, except on the dough cycle.

> ½ C warm milk
>
> ¼ C orange juice
>
> juice of ½ lemon
>
> 4 C flour
>
> 1 C sugar
>
> ½ tsp salt
>
> 2 tsp yeast
>
> ¾ C melted butter
>
> **Add at beeper or last 5 minutes:**
>
> ½ C seedless white raisins soaked in marsala wine
>
> ¼ C pine nuts
>
> ⅛ C peeled pistachios
>
> 1 T fennel seeds
>
> ½ C candied fruit (finely chopped)

Place the liquids (except the butter) and dry ingredients into the bread pan and start on the dough cycle. Run it about 10 minutes. Stop the machine. Add the melted butter. Start it again on the fruit or raisin bread cycle, this time. When the beeper sounds, add the fruit and nuts. If you don't have a beeper to inform you when to add fruit, add the stuff during the last 5 minutes of the kneading cycle.

Challah Alla Machine

This is an adaptation of Craig Claiborne's adaptation of Mrs. Sarah Schecht's recipe for what all agreed to be the best challah recipe anywhere. Can be made as regular loaf of bread in the bread machine. Go to the dough section of the book for the better, braided version.

1 lb	1½ lb & 2 lb
5 oz warm water	1 C warm water
1 medium egg*	2 medium eggs*
2¼ C flour	4 C flour
⅛ tsp baking powder	¼ tsp baking powder
⅛ tsp cinnamon	¼ tsp cinnamon
¾ tsp salt	1½ tsp salt
¼ tsp vanilla	½ tsp vanilla
1½ T corn oil margarine	2½ T corn oil margarine
1½ T sugar	2½ T sugar
1½ tsp yeast	2 T yeast

*See my comments on egg measurement in ingredients section (p. 16).

Kickapoo Joy Bread

I won't go into detail about the name of this bread; it's too involved. Those of you who remember the cartoon strip *Li'l Abner* will recall the name. If you, or someone you know, has a genuine weight problem, they'll love this. It is, to be perfectly frank, a real health bread.

> 1 very ripe banana, mashed,
>   plus orange juice to make 1 C liquid
>
> 2 C flour
>
> 1 C whole wheat flour
>
> 2 T brown sugar
>
> 1 tsp lemon juice
>
> 1 tsp cinnamon
>
> ¼ tsp ground cloves
>
> ¼ tsp ginger
>
> 1 tsp salt
>
> 1½ tsp yeast

You'll need one really overripe, black banana. That's when they're best for cooking. Start by putting the banana in the measuring cup and mushing it up well. Because this loaf doesn't rise that high, you can make it in all 3 machines. Just wait until you smell it baking.

Lydia D'Anna's Hangover Bread

This seems a fitting thing with which to end this section: My daughter Lydia made a loaf of bread in her new bread machine. She mistakenly added a tablespoon full of salt instead of the teaspoon called for in the original recipe. Before eating it, she took it to her friend Kathy. When they tried the bread, it was very salty. Kathy, whose father is a doctor (and so Kathy seems privy to such things), recognized it immediately as a pretty good thing to eat when you're nursing a hangover. I suggested the optional bitters. I mean, if you're fighting a hangover, you need all the ammunition you can get. Lydia says this is great heaped with preserves. I say slice it thinly, toast it, and spread it with cheese.

1 lb	1½ lb	2 lb
5 oz water	6 oz water	7 oz water
2 oz milk	3 oz milk	½ C milk
2½ C flour	3¼ C flour	4 C flour
¼ tsp Angostura bitters*	½ tsp Angostura bitters*	¾ tsp Angostura bitters*
1 tsp sugar	1½ tsp sugar	2 tsp sugar
1 T shortening	1½ T shortening	2 T shortening
1 T salt	2 T salt	2½ T salt
1½ tsp yeast	2 tsp yeast	2½ tsp yeast

*Optional.

Porter Bread

Here is a good dark, rich bread. It needn't be made with porter; a good, dark bock, or black-and-tan beer will do it. You don't have to worry about serving it to Uncle Arthur, if he is still on the wagon; the alcohol dissipates in the cooking. It is a good idea to stir the beer to help flatten it some before adding to the pan. This loaf may be done on the regular or rapid rise, or even on the dough cycle.

1 lb	1½ lb	2 lb
⅞ C porter	1 C porter	1¼ C porter
1 oz molasses*	¼ C molasses*	⅓ C molasses*
1 T soft butter	2 T soft butter	2½ T soft butter
1½ C flour	2 C flour	2½ C flour
¾ C whole wheat flour	1¼ C whole wheat flour	1¾ C whole wheat flour
1 tsp salt	1½ tsp salt	2 tsp salt
1½ tsp yeast	2 tsp yeast	2½ tsp yeast

* You can substitute dark corn syrup for the molasses.

The Dough Setting

Dough is unbaked bread (or rolls, or pizza). Making dough had been, until about 10 years ago, the hard part of making bread. With the invention of the bread machine it became the easy part. With the bread machine, dough became again, as it had been for centuries, readily available. Up until the liberations of the 20th century, dough had been one of the primary responsibilities of women, who were known as "ladies," or kneaders of dough. It was a term of honor and respect.

The recipes in this section of the book are designed to be prepared in the bread machine on the dough setting, finished by hand, and baked in the oven. You can either use the dough that comes out of the bread machine immediately, or put it in a covered bowl or plastic storage bag and keep it in the refrigerator to use when the spirit moves you. After a day or so, the dough begins to get a little sour; some detect a slight fragrance of beer.

From that stored dough, you can make bread or rolls or pizza. Further, you don't have to use all of it at one time. Leaving some, and adding to it, you have the basis of a nice sourdough starter (see page 121 for more about this). So if there are just the two of you for dinner, take enough for a few dinner rolls and leave the rest. When the dough supply gets down, you whip up another batch and add it to the stored batch. I've not been successful combining the two separate doughs by just kneading by hand. What I do is toss the dough from the fridge in with the fresh dough as it is being kneaded in the machine. I heat the older dough in the microwave for 2 to 3 minutes on the lowest setting. It is a good idea to wait until the new batch of dough has been kneading in the machine for about 10 minutes before combining them.

Below are a couple of basic recipes for Refrigerated Dough. From the two recipes that follow, you can make many different kinds of bread or rolls. This dough will last several days in the fridge, and it is there whenever you need it. You may notice there is little or no shortening in these two recipes. Once the shortening gets cold, it will be more resistant to rising and inhibit the yeast's development and action. Knead a little shortening into the dough when you are ready to shape it. The shortening can depend on the final product: butter for sweet breakfast rolls, olive oil for pizza, lard for nice hamburger or hot dog rolls, or margarine for a curious but good texture, or even apple sauce, if you're avoiding fat.

Cold dough fresh out of the fridge is rather easy to work with, but it can take at least an hour or two before it is ready to bake in the oven. To speed this up, put the amount of dough you want to use in a bowl, cover with a damp cloth or paper, and put it in the microwave on the lowest setting. You'll want to do this for only a minute or two on one side; then flip it over and do the other side for only a minute. This will begin warming the dough and wake up the yeast.

Refrigerated Dough #1

¾ C water

2 C flour*

1 tsp sugar

1 tsp salt

1 tsp yeast

*If you have it, a tablespoon of rye flour helps the flavor.

This dough will sour rather nicely, and is best for savory or basic rolls or loaves. It is a pretty good pizza dough, too.

Refrigerated Dough #2 (Sweeter)

This is a sweeter dough, good for perhaps more things (including pizza, if you like a slightly sweeter dough).

¾ C water

¼ C milk

1 tsp shortening

2¾ C flour

1 tsp sugar

1 tsp salt

1¼ tsp yeast

Review of Dough Handling

I hate those cookbooks that seem patronizing or talk down to you, but at the risk of doing so, bear with me. If you're experienced, you may not need any of the following. If you're not, or just somewhat lacking in confidence, let me give you a hand.

Your dough should feel kind of soft and almost sticky, almost alive. Actually it is alive. The dough from your bread machine is as good or better than handmade dough. The climate will affect the dough to some extent. On a rainy or humid day, the dough will feel more sticky and a bit yucchy to work with, while on dry cool days, a bit harder. But don't worry about all of this; the machine has done most of the work. So let's take a quick review of the fine art of kneading.

All You Need to Know About Kneading

Kneading helps determine the texture of the finished loaf. Since the bread machine has actually made the dough, all you are going to do in this final kneading is the final finishing, adding the final shape and purpose. The recipes in the next couple of sections require a minute or two of kneading, mainly to press the air out of the dough and strengthen the structure of the gluten. You don't want to bang the dough, which might break the strands of gluten. You only want to press them together, and give the expanding fermenting yeast something to press against.

Just in case you've never kneaded dough, or it has been so long that you've forgotten all about it, let's have a brief refresher:

1. Spread a little flour on a work surface.

2. Dump the dough onto it.

3. Press all the gas (good old carbon dioxide) out of the dough. If the dough is too sticky to work with, if it actually sticks to your hands, sprinkle a little — just a little — more flour on it until it doesn't stick to your hands.

4. Flatten the lump into a round disc.

5. Fold the disc in half and press it flat again.

6. Repeat steps 4 and 5, continuing for a minute or so.

Sometimes the dough will become too lively to work and will resist your kneading it. In fact, you'll find you can't knead it at all. The answer is to let it rest for about 5 to 10 minutes. It will settle down, and then you can continue to shape the dough for whatever.

On Letting the Final Product Rise Before Baking

Almost all cookbooks (not just the bread machine books) tell you to let the rolls (or loaf) rise in a warm (90°F), draft-free place, until double in bulk.

I have noticed, however, that dough left in the refrigerator overnight also rises. Your kitchen is probably a warm enough place. If it isn't, simply turn your oven on the lowest setting for a minute or two; then turn it off again. Be sure to turn the oven off! Then turn the oven light on and put the rolls or loaves in, give them a quick spray of warm water, and they will rise nicely in less than an hour.

Italian Fries

> Refrigerated Dough #1 (see p. 61)
>
> grated parmesan cheese
>
> cooking oil or other shortening
>
> tomato sauce (optional)

We'll start what has to be the simplest of dough recipes, and quite rewarding, for these strips of fried dough with grated cheese and sauce. These are good little things if you have one of those handy electric deep-fat fryers, and no less good if you don't and have to heat the fat on the stove (to 350°F).

Take a batch of Refrigerated Dough #1. Roll it out flat, really flat, ¼ inch thick. Cut it in ½-inch-wide strips about 3 inches long. Let the strips rest while you bring the cooking oil up to temperature.

Drop the strips into the hot oil a few at a time, 3 or 4 or whatever the container will hold comfortably, and fry until done — a couple of minutes. Remove from the oil, and set on a rack over paper towels. While they are still hot, sprinkle them with grated parmesan cheese. You can eat these instead of French fries with hamburgers, or just dip in a tomato sauce and eat. Fry up a hog's load, and eat while watching a movie and drinking beer or wine.

The next morning, there's the container with the fat already to go again. Here is something as easy as the above.

Elephant Ears

They can also look like lion ears, or rabbit ears, depending on how you cut them. They are another delicious fried dough. A breakfast treat, served with cinnamon sugar. Although you can use Refrigerated Dough #2, you can try the following recipe which I came up with in a fit of sudden inspiration. With the inclusion of egg, it is more resistant to fat penetration.

⅔ C water

¼ C milk

1 egg

1 tsp shortening

2¾ C flour

1 T sugar

1 tsp salt

1 tsp yeast

For topping: cinnamon and sugar

Prepare the dough on the dough setting. Roll the dough out flat, really flat, ¼ inch thick. Cut 3-inch circles, or 3-inch triangles, or random shapes, for that matter. Let the shapes rest for 10 to 15 minutes while you heat the fat to 350°F.

Drop them into the hot oil a few at a time, 3 or 4 or whatever the container will hold comfortably, and fry until done — a couple of minutes. Remove from the oil, and set on a rack over paper towels. While they are still hot, sprinkle them with a mixture of cinnamon and sugar. Eat them while sipping a tasty breakfast beverage.

Basic Rolls

For those of you who've never made rolls before, let's start with recipe Refrigerated Dough #1 (page 61), which will be good, especially if you are having spaghetti tonight. Presuming the dough is in the fridge and nice and cold, first spread a little flour on the counter, remove the dough from the storage bag, and press all the air out of it. Put maybe a tablespoon of olive oil on the dough; then follow the above instructions for kneading (page 62). This should take only a minute or two — really.

Roll the dough into a nice rope, about an inch in diameter. Then cut 2- to 3-inch lengths of the rope. Those are now rolls. Spread a little cornmeal (if you haven't any cornmeal, spread a little oil) on a baking sheet. Place the rolls on the sheet, and put it in a warm place to rise. You are going to let them rise anywhere from 30 minutes to an hour. Set your oven to 400°F, about 15 minutes before you are ready to bake. Before you put the rolls in the oven, take a very sharp knife and put a ¼-inch-deep slit in the top of each one. These are called jets; they help the rolls rise higher. Slip the sheet into the oven and bake 15 minutes. That's it. You should have about 8 deluxe, gourmet rolls!

Dinner Rolls

Using Refrigerated Dough #2, do the same thing as for Basic Rolls, except knead in a tablespoon of melted butter or margarine. Roll out the dough into a ½-inch-diameter rope. Cut 4-inch lengths and then tie the lengths into loose knots. Place them on a cookie sheet, and let them rise only about a half hour. Then take an egg and beat it fairly well. Add a tablespoon of water and a dash of salt; then brush the rolls with this. Bake in a 400°F oven for 15 minutes for wonderful dinner rolls.

Yes. It is just that simple. Total time, in case you figure that sort of thing, is 2 minutes to load the bread machine, 2 minutes to dump the finished product into a storage bag, and 5 minutes to make the rolls. Less than 10 minutes. Cost? Very inexpensive.

Making Loaves from Refrigerated Dough

To make loaves of the two different Refrigerated Dough recipes given above, you simply follow the instructions up to the final shaping. At that point, you simply make up your mind how you want the final shape: round, oblong, flat and round, a long baguette, et cetera. The loaves can be baked in pans, and there you can let your imagination go for a fling. Try rolling the dough in a rope sufficiently long to put into a bundt pan. Or, if you have a decorative pan, make a heart, egg, castle. You get the idea. For Refrigerated Dough #1, cut a ¼-inch-deep slit (jet) into the final loaf before putting it into the oven. And either loaf goes well with an egg wash. Bake loaves from both recipes for at least a half hour, Refrigerator Dough #1 at 400°F, Refrigerated Dough #2 at 350°F.

Next, let's jump right into a more advanced, but not really difficult, recipe which I regard as a national treasure.

Sarah Schecht's Challah

I thought the recipe I had been using for challah in my two previous books was pretty near the last word on the subject. Then I came across an old Craig Claiborne book of his favorite recipes. I realized again how true was the maxim on recipes: "There's always another way to do it." Reminds me of the story about Brahms hearing someone play one of his piano pieces in a most peculiar way. His response was: "So, it can be played that way too."

Well, in spite of my cavalier way with recipes, and my encouraging readers to be the same way, I tried this recipe and found that it is indeed better than the one I've been using, so follow this one as I've given it.

Credit should be given here to Mr. Claiborne's source, Mrs. Sarah Schecht, who was responsible for what all agreed to be the best challah anywhere. I've tried Claiborne's adaptation of her recipe and it is good. But in his discussion of how the good lady made the bread, he mentioned one ingredient she was using when he visited her; then he called for a different one in the recipe. Mrs. Schecht used margarine. Mr. Claiborne called for oil. And since I have been experimenting with margarine anyway, and because I've been enjoying the texture that margarine adds to certain breads, I specify what the master used. I adapted the recipe for two sizes in the machine-baked recipes section. It is quite good if you just load the machine and bake it as is. But here we make it very close to the way Mrs. Schecht did it, by braiding it. It can be prepared in any bread machine.

Sara Schecht's Challah

4½ C flour

1¼ C warm water

¼ tsp baking powder

¼ tsp cinnamon

1½ tsp salt

½ tsp vanilla

2 medium eggs

⅓ C corn oil margarine

⅓ C sugar

1 T yeast

Set the machine for the dough cycle. Combine the liquid ingredients in the pan. Now combine all the dry ingredients and add to the pan, and start the machine. Remove dough from the machine when done, onto a floured surface. Press all the air out of the loaf and let it rest for 10 to 15 minutes. Divide the dough into four equal pieces. Shape each one into a rope about 1 inch in diameter and about 14 inches long. Lay the 4 pieces down one on top of the other. Pinch the 4 ends together at the top. Now braid them loosely, like you daughter's hair. At the end, pinch the strand ends together. Let rise for 45 minutes to 1 hour. Bake in 350°F oven for 35 to 40 minutes.

Pretzels

I'm guessing that many of you are going to think that making pretzels is something hard to do. I'm writing to you from Pennsylvania, where it seems pretzels recently have become the #1 export (well, maybe not exactly #1, but pretty high up there, nonetheless). Suffice it to say they make an awful lot of pretzels in Pennsylvania, so it is only fitting that a book originating here should include a pretzel recipe or two. Originally pretzels were made from the ever-present dough. They are rather easy to make.

The pretzels for which the state is best known are those soft pretzels they sell in Philadelphia, and now increasingly around the country, frozen, if you will! We'll start with a soft pretzel recipe.

Philadelphia Soft Pretzels

Makes about a dozen 6-inch pretzels.

> 1¼ C warm water
>
> 4 C flour
>
> 1 tsp sugar
>
> ½ tsp salt
>
> 1 tsp yeast
>
> **For egg wash:**
>
> 1 egg, beaten well
>
> 1 T water
>
> dash of salt
>
> **For sprinkling:** coarse salt

Prepare on the dough cycle. When done, remove to a floured surface, and push the remaining air out of the dough. Let it rest for a few minutes. The easiest way I have found to do this is to roll the dough out into a rope sufficiently long to cut into 12 equal pieces that are 12 inches long. Of course you can estimate the size you want. Take a piece of this dough, roll it in your hands to make a rope about a foot long; let it hang like an upside down "U." Lay it on the table, cross the two ends about halfway up, twist them once. Then fold the ends down so they meet the curve of the "U" and you've got it. Pinch together where ends overlap.

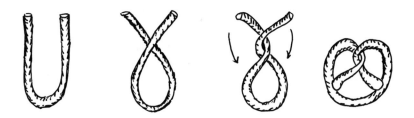

Place on a lightly greased (sprayed) baking sheet and let rise about 30 minutes, or until not quite doubled in bulk. Brush with the egg wash. Sprinkle the tops generously with coarse salt and bake in a hot (475°F) oven for about 10 minutes.

To get hard pretzels, when you remove the pretzels from the oven, turn off the oven, let it cool for maybe 15 minutes; then put the pretzels back in on the oven rack and let them stay there for several hours. When you take them out of the oven the second time, you'll have those tooth-breakers that people pay too much for in Lancaster County, Pennsylvania — what we call stale pretzels.

A Justifiably Famous Pretzel

There is a justifiably famous pretzel emanating from Lancaster County, Pennsylvania, which can be reasonably duplicated. *(Makes about a dozen 6-inch pretzels)*

1¼ C warm water	4 C flour
1 T sugar	½ tsp salt
1 tsp yeast	

For dipping before baking:

3 T melted butter	2 T melted margarine
1 tsp sugar	1 tsp salt

Combine the 4 dipping ingredients in a wide-bottom bowl, something akin to a cereal or soup bowl.

Prepare the dough on the dough cycle. When done, remove to a floured surface, and push the remaining air out of the dough. Let it rest for 10 minutes. Roll the dough out to a rope sufficiently long to cut into 12 equal pieces that are 12 inches long. Roll each piece into a rope about ½ inch in diameter; then form into a pretzel (see Soft Pretzels shaping instructions). Dip each pretzel into the dipping mixture. Place on a lightly greased (sprayed) baking sheet and let rise about 30 minutes, or until not quite doubled in bulk. Bake in a fairly hot (400°F) oven for about 10 to 12 minutes.

Oyster Crackers (or Soup Balls)

These should stop that disgusting habit of breaking one's crackers into the soup. (And your kids can throw them at each other; lots of uses for them.) But mainly, they taste good.

> 1 C water
>
> 3 C flour
>
> 1 tsp lard (or vegetable shortening)
>
> ½ tsp salt
>
> 1 tsp sugar
>
> ½ tsp baking soda
>
> 1½ tsp yeast

Prepare on the dough cycle. Remove when done, push all the air out of the dough, and put in an ungreased bowl. Refrigerate until thoroughly chilled, an hour or so. There are two or three ways to proceed:

Method 1. Roll out until the dough is a ¼-inch-thick oblong. Cut the dough criss-cross into half-inch squares (yes, I said half-inch squares).

Method 2. Roll out into a half-inch diameter rope, and cut it every half-inch.

Method 3. Tear off little bits from the dough ball, and roll each into a small ball in your hands. Flatten to ½-inch thickness.

Then separate them on a baking sheet and let them rise for half an hour. Spray with water and bake in a 400°F oven for 10 minutes.

Pandolce Genovese

This recipe also is included in the section for recipes baked in the bread machine. It can be made in the machine, but it is better made on the dough cycle. Traditionally it is baked in a fancy or decorative pan, but a large, round stainless steel bowl is good. It can also be done, and perhaps more wisely, in two or three smaller decorative pans. It would make a delightful Christmas gift, much easier than traditional Christmas cookies. It is similar to that other holiday favorite from Italy, Panettone. It is not from Turin or Milan, but Genoa; hence it is called Pandolce Genovese.

½ C warm milk

¼ C orange juice

juice of ½ lemon

4 C flour

1 C sugar

½ tsp salt

1 T fennel seeds

1½ tsp yeast

¾ C melted butter

Add at fruit beeper:

¼ C pine nuts

⅛ C peeled pistachios

1 C (scant) seedless white raisins,
     soaked in marsala wine

4 oz candied fruit (finely chopped)

Place the liquids (except the melted butter) into the bread pan. Add the dry ingredients. Start the bread machine and let it knead for about 10 minutes. Stop the machine. Add the melted butter, and start it again from the beginning; you'll want it on the dough cycle this time.

An Easy Coffee or Breakfast Cake

It's simple to make tasty cake. You can make the dough the night before and chill it. Then bake as cakes the next morning. The original name for this cake was a *stiacciata* cake — that means "squashed cake." You'll need two flat cake pans, ideally 8 inches × 12 inches. If you haven't two, find something about 200 square inches. Originally the cake was baked in a 12 × 20 inch pan.

4 C flour

⅓ C sugar**

½ tsp salt

1¼ C orange juice*

2 eggs

1 stick of butter, softened
   (or ½ stick each of butter and margarine)

1½ tsp yeast

<u>Also:</u>

butter or oil for baking pans

confectioners' sugar for coating

*If you don't have orange juice, squeeze the juice of half a lemon into water to total 1¼ C.
**If you are using the lemon water, increase sugar to ½ cup.

Because of the amount of fat, you'll want to get the gluten good and strong first of all. So first put the flour, sugar, salt, and juice into the bread pan, and on the dough cycle, run the machine for 10 to 15 minutes. Now add the eggs and the softened butter. Add the yeast. Start the machine over on the dough cycle and run to completion. When done, grease the baking pans (or pan) with butter or oil, and divide the dough for the pans. Flatten the dough and fit in the pans. Cover the pans and leave for an hour to an hour and a half. It will take time for this to rise because of the fat (eggs and butter).

Bake in a 400°F oven for 20 to 25 minutes, or until golden. Turn the cakes onto a wire rack to cool. When cool, turn the cakes over, exposing the creases from the rack, and dust with confectioners' sugar.

Moravian Sugar Cakes

In the late 18th and early 19th century, an excellent Protestant sect, the Moravians, settled in the northeastern part of Pennsylvania. There they spread about this fine fertile land their rich culture, a reserved and intelligent religion, superb music, and the following recipe.

There is a difference of opinion at the outset here. My wife, not one to be trifled with, says they are done as a coffee cake in a 9-inch cake pan. I have bought them at Auchenbach's Bakery (a bakery so good, by the way, that people come from miles around just to stand on their doorstep) in the thriving little city of Bird In Hand, and they were actually little cakes. The cakes do keep well, so if the recipe seems too much to eat in one sitting, wrap one of the cakes in waxed paper, then aluminum foil, and freeze it. Here, then, are both ways.

½ C potato water*

¼ C milk

1 egg

2 T mashed potatoes (or 1 T instant potatoes)

3 T shortening**

2½ C all-purpose flour

¼ C sugar

1 tsp salt

1¼ tsp yeast

For topping:

½ C brown sugar mixed with 2 tsp cinnamon

¼ C melted butter

*If you haven't saved your potato water, you can use just regular water.
**Auchenbach's uses vegetable shortening. I use lard.

Prepare dough on the dough cycle. When done, use either version 1 or 2 (page 74) to finish.

Version #1: Press the dough into a couple of greased 8-inch cake pans. (You can use 9-inch pans, but the cakes won't be as high.) Spray the tops with water and let rise in a warm place for nearly an hour.

Make indentations about the size of the first joint of your pointer finger and an inch apart in the top of the cakes. My wife does this by making her hand like a claw, then dabbing her fingers as noted above. Then, using a teaspoon, spoon the sugar and cinnamon mixture into the holes. Drizzle ¼ cup melted butter over the top of the cakes. Bake in a 350°F oven for about 20 minutes, or until golden brown. Remove from the cake pan and cool.

Version #2: Cut three ½-inch pieces off a stick of butter. Divide each piece into 4 parts. When the dough is done, roll it into a nice long log. Divide it into 12 more or less equal pieces. Roll each piece into a ball; then flatten it into a cake. Now make an indentation,about the size of the first joint of your pointer finger, in the middle of the cake; put a piece of the butter in the middle, then spoon a teaspoon of the cinnamon and sugar topping over the butter. Spray the tops with water, and let the cakes rise in a warm place for nearly an hour. Bake in a 350°F oven for about 20 minutes. Cool on a rack and eat.

Babka

A traditional Polish festive loaf. More of a cake even than the Italian Pandolce Genovese. There are probably as many recipes for babka as there are people to make them. I found two versions, and they confirmed my oft-stated position on recipes. One recipe has 3 egg yolks, and chopped almonds spread on top before cooking. Another has 8 egg yolks, and rum or brandy poured over the top before it cools; then it is well-sprinkled with confectioners' sugar when cool. Well, try this recipe. You may safely be cavalier with this recipe. If you haven't 5 egg yolks, use 3 or 4. Try half margarine and half butter. You can skip the lemon peel and try a 1½ teaspoons of almond extract and add chopped almonds with the raisins.

I'm including a nice old-country touch: poppy-seed filling (page 76), as still another option instead of raisins. Or you can just use the recipe as I've adapted it to all sizes of the bread machine. Bake it in an angel food cake pan or bundt pan. (A 12-inch-long loaf pan might be nice.)

Babka

1 C milk	2 tsp yeast
3 C (plus) flour	½ tsp salt
⅓ C sugar	6 T butter (softened)
5 egg yolks, at room temperature	½ C golden raisins
1 T grated lemon peel	1 oz rum, brandy, or Grand Marnier
confectioners' sugar	

Begin by warming the milk; then put it and the yeast in the bottom of the bread pan. Let it sit for 10 minutes or so. Now add the flour and salt and start the bread machine. Set the machine for the dough setting. Let it run for 10 to 15 minutes. What you are doing is building up the gluten in the dough. All the butter and eggs will inhibit this.

Stop the machine and remove the dough ball and set aside. Put the butter in the bottom of the bread pan; then the ⅓ C sugar. Start the machine again. Let the butter and sugar become well blended. Then add the egg yolks, more or less one at a time. Add the lemon rind. Let all of this mix well.

Cut the dough ball into 4 pieces and one by one add to the mixing. Check to see just how wet the dough is. If it pulls away from the sides as it mixes, it is fine. If it is soupy, add more flour until it does pull easily from the sides. Let the machine complete its job.

When complete, put the dough on a well-floured work surface, flatten and stretch out so that you can roll it, and put it in a round bundt or tube pan. Add the raisins and pat them into the dough or use poppy seed filling. Fold the dough to cover the raisins, and lay it in the well-buttered pan.

Let rise to at least doubled in bulk (45 minutes did it for me), and bake in a 375°F oven for 35 minutes. Remove from pan to a cooling rack, and pour or brush on the liquor. Cover with a cloth and let cool. Then sprinkle with confectioners' sugar.

Poppy Seed Filling for Babka

As with babka recipes, it seems poppy seed fillings are numerous as can be. In my own cookbook collection, I have maybe a half-dozen. Here's what I developed for this babka recipe.

½ C poppy seeds

1 to 2 T milk

1 tsp lemon juice

2 T soft butter

1 to 2 T dried cake or bread crumbs

1 tsp grated lemon rind

½ tsp cinnamon

¼ tsp ground cloves

¼ tsp nutmeg

Grind or mash the poppy seeds and milk in a mortar or bowl with a pestle or heavy spoon and mix well together until it's a soft paste. Add the rest of the ingredients and mix together well. To add to babka, first roll out the babka to the desired length. Spread the filling lengthwise on the dough; then fold the dough over it. Place it in the pan and let rise; proceed as above (see babka recipe).

Olive Bread

You can add the ingredients of this wonderful snacking loaf, and just bake it in the machine. If you do bake this in the bread machine, select the setting which will beep to let you know when to add the olives. Otherwise, add the olives five minutes before the machine is through kneading the dough. Or, much better, you can do it as I suggest below. If you do it my way, you can use just half the amount of dough for baking and freeze the other half for later use. It is wonderful for a deep-dish pizza, and an excellent accompaniment to a simple spaghetti dinner, or even just a salad.

¼ C olive oil

2 T fresh rosemary (or 1 tsp dried)

1 clove garlic, chopped fine

1 C water

3½ C flour

½ C rye flour

1 T sugar

1½ tsp salt

2 tsp yeast

At the beeper, or 5 minutes before the end of kneading, add:

1 C mixed black, brown and green olives, chopped*

*The better the olives, the better the bread.

Start by heating the olive oil in a saucepan; add the rosemary and garlic and saute for 2 or 3 minutes. You don't want the garlic to get brown, at least not too brown, anyway.

Now add this oil and garlic to the bread pan. Wash out the pan in which you just sauteed with the cup of warm water (waste not, want not) and add that to the bread pan. Add the dry ingredients to the pan, except for the olives. Set on the dough setting and let it go. If your machine doesn't beep for additions, add the olives 5 minutes before the machine is through kneading the dough.

Remove the dough. Press all the air out of the dough and let it rest for 5 to 10 minutes. Now you have two choices, described on the next page.

Method 1: Divide the dough in two and knead it a for a minute, flatten it out into a round, and fit it into a well-oiled round pan. I use an old 9-inch round, 2-inch deep cake pan. If you go by that basic measurement, approximately 130 cubic inches, you can pick your own pan. Or, if you have the more common 8-inch round, 1½-inch deep cake pan, you can use that, but you had better divide the dough into three parts, so you can have more than one loaf. Too much dough in too small a pan will make the dough push past the lid as it bakes.

Once in the pan, let the dough rest for a half an hour, and heat the oven to 400°F. Place a cover on the pan, such as a round pizza pan, or something, and put a weight on it — a heavy frying pan or a red brick. You want a good 3 to 5 pounds. You want to keep the bread from rising while it is baking, and also to keep much of the moisture in the bread as it bakes. Bake for 30 minutes in a 400°F oven.

Method 2: If you have a 2-inch-deep, 9- or 10-inch round pan, flatten the dough into a round, and put it in the pan. Again, you want that cover on the pan and in this case you definitely want to restrict the rising of the bread with the heavy weight, as in Method 1. Bake for 30 minutes in a 400°F oven.

When done, remove to a cooling rack, slice in narrow slices; you should be able to get a dozen, maybe even 16 slices. Wonderful with salad. Serve it with dry red house wine, while listening to Albeniz' "Iberia" and looking out over the Mediterranean. Ahhh!

The Pullman Loaves

You can buy Pullman loaf pans either from better professional kitchen supply outlets or from several different catalogs. They cost between $30 and $40 as of this writing, which may seem expensive, but when you consider the product of the pans, they are certainly worth it.

Pullman loaves are particularly wonderful if you have a large family, throw lots of parties, or own a restaurant. Pullman loaves keep well. You can put one into a plastic bag, refrigerate it and keep it for several days, or freeze it and keep it for several months. I am convinced that this is the best all around bread you can bake.

The finished loaves are square and long, about 4 × 4 × 13 inches. The pans hold a 5-cup (of flour) bread recipe. The dough to fill such a pan can be made even in a 1½ lb loaf machine. The pan has a sliding, rather tightly fitting top, which is closed when the bread is baking. This restricts the rising of the bread, and the dissipation of steam as the loaf bakes. Because the moisture stays in the loaf, it is rather dense and so, easier to slice thin.

It is a method for making a loaf of bread simply unequaled by any other, at least for toast or sandwiches. The method of baking which inspired the Pullman loaf pan is French in origin. This type loaf of bread is also called a *pain de mie*, which means "bread without a cover" or "without a crust." The texture of the bread is much firmer than other loaves. The loaf is flat on all 4 sides and at both ends, so it is much easier to slice off the crust.

I am including three recipes for use in the Pullman pan. All three recipes are for use on the dough cycle of the 1½ or 2 lb bread machine. In the 1½ lb machine, by the time the dough is ready for putting in the Pullman pan, it will be forcing up the top of the machine. Not to worry.

James Beard suggests you can duplicate the effect of the Pullman loaf by putting a cover on a regular bread pan and weighting it down with bricks. It is the steam from the baking, arrested in the bread, that contributes to its wonderful texture and staying power.

You may not be able to use these recipes in the small (1-lb) bread machines. I'm not sure the motors will take the amount of ingredients in the recipe. But they might. You can check the specifications, or even call the toll-free number that comes with most machines to inquire.

A Pretty Perfect Pullman

¾ C water	¾ C milk
¼ C lard	5 C flour
2 T sugar	1 T salt
3 tsp yeast	

Prepare on the dough cycle. When done, remove to a floured surface, and push the remaining air out of the dough. Let it rest for a few minutes. Shape it into a log sufficiently long to fit into the pan. Spray the loaf with water and close the pan, all but maybe an inch. Let it rise in a warm place for about three-quarters of an hour, or until it nearly fills the pan. Slide the lid closed and place into an oven heated to 350°F. Bake for 40 minutes. You'll have trouble believing bread can smell this good.

Perfect Ham-and-Cheese or Roast Beef Sandwich Bread*

1½ C water	¼ C lard or bacon drippings
4 C bread or unbleached white flour	1 C rye flour
1 T brown sugar	½ tsp dill weed
1 tsp caraway seed	½ tsp ground black pepper
1½ T salt	2½ tsp yeast

Prepare on the dough cycle. When done, remove to a floured surface, and push the remaining air out of the dough. Let it rest for a few minutes. Shape it into a log sufficiently long to fit into the pan. Spray the loaf with water and close the pan, all but maybe an inch. Let it rise in a warm place for about three-quarters of an hour, or until it nearly fills the pan. Slide the lid closed and place in an oven heated to 350°F. Bake for 40 minutes.

*It's not bad for turkey sandwiches, either.

Mr. Beard's Toasting White*

I suppose Beard's use of butter is no worse than my use of lard. If you are still a Fatophobe, you'll want to pass on this loaf. The two big differences between butter and lard are the flavor and the texture. This is another example of a breakfast loaf supreme. It needn't be made in a Pullman loaf pan. It could be baked as a large round loaf.

5½ C flour	1 T sugar
1½ T+ salt	6 T unsalted butter
1½ C warm water	3 tsp yeast

First combine and sift all the dry ingredients, except the yeast. Put about 3 cups of these sifted ingredients into a bowl. Using a pastry cutter, cut the butter into the dry ingredients in the bowl. Set aside.

Now, put the water into the bread pan, with the other 2½ cups of dry ingredients and the yeast. Select the dough cycle and start the machine. Let the machine run for 10 minutes. (What you're doing is building up a lot of gluten before it has to contend with all that butter.) Stop the machine. Let the dough rest for about 10 minutes. Add the dry ingredients with the butter cut in to the resting dough in the machine. Now you are going to start all over again. Select the dough cycle again, and start.

This time let it run to completion, on the dough cycle. When done, remove the dough from the bread pan onto a floured surface, and push the remaining air out of the dough. Let it rest for about 10 minutes. Then place it in a buttered bowl, turning it so that the dough ball is completely covered with butter, and let it rise for at least an hour in a warm place.

Remove the dough to a floured surface. Push all the air out of the dough ball; let it rest for 10 minutes. Shape the dough to fit into the Pullman pan, if you are using one. Spray the loaf with water and close the pan, all but maybe an inch. Let the dough rise in a warm place for another hour, or until it nearly fills the pan. Heat the oven to 400°F. Slide the lid of the pan closed and place it in that 400°F oven. Immediately reduce the oven temperature to 350°F and bake for 30 minutes.

After 30 minutes, remove the loaf from the pan and put the loaf back in the oven for another 10 minutes, until (as Mr. Beard says) "the bread is beautiful in color and sounds hollow when you rap it." Let it cool thoroughly on a rack before slicing. You'll bless me for this.

*As interpreted by Mr. Wanless.

Absolutely Delicious Whole Wheat Sandwich Bread

½ C water

1 C milk

¼ C corn oil margarine

3 C bread flour or unbleached white flour

2 C whole wheat flour

2 T brown sugar or honey

1 T salt

2½ tsp yeast

Prepare on the dough cycle. When done, remove to a floured surface, and push the remaining air out of the dough. Let it rest for a few minutes. Shape it into a log sufficiently long to fit into the pan. Spray the loaf with water and close the pan, all but maybe an inch. Let it rise in a warm place for about ¾ hour, or until it nearly fills the pan. Slide the lid closed and place into an oven heated to 350°F. Bake for 40 minutes.

Recipes for Meals

Well, of course, most of these aren't really meals. But I'm sure you've heard something to the effect: "Why, that bread is a meal in itself." I have had bread, in fact, that was a meal unto itself. A loaf of that splendid, hearth-baked New York Italian bread comes to mind. My wife's version of the ancient repast Garlic Bread is another. But breads as meals, I think, feature the bread as the base or entree, and what is loaded on or in it is the dressing, as it were. Probably the most elemental of the breads as meals — aside of course, from the abovenoted — is this ancient focaccia.

Focaccia alla Salvia

You've seen whole books dedicated to focaccia. Focaccia is just flavored bread, baked in a shape that makes an excellent platform for heaping stuff on it and eating, rather like an open-faced sandwich. Or, if you're so inclined, eat it with nothing on it and enjoy it just as it is, with a good beer or wine. The instructions I use for focaccia are really the basis for a number of similar bread meals. Throughout this section we'll keep referring to them.

> 4 C flour
>
> 1¼ C warm water
>
> 2 tsp salt
>
> 1½ tsp yeast
>
> **After first kneading cycle, add:**
>
> ¼ C olive oil
>
> 6 to 12 fresh sage leaves, finely chopped*

*Or a rounded teaspoon of dried ground sage.

Select the dough cycle; place the first 4 ingredients in the bread pan. Start the machine and let it run through the first kneading cycle only. If your machine doesn't keep you informed with what it's doing (kneading, rest, 1st rise, et cetera), stop the machine after it has completed its kneading cycle. You can tell by the fact that the machine is silent. (If you forget to stop the machine, that's all right. It won't hurt it to run the whole cycle.

The original recipe from which I have adapted this said to let it rise for 1 to 2 hours after kneading it for 30 minutes!)

Now, add the olive oil and the sage leaves to the dough in the bread pan, and start the machine again. Let it run the whole cycle this time (or again). When it's done, remove to a floured surface, punch it down, and let it rest for about 10 minutes. Roll the dough out until it is flat and maybe ¼-inch thick. Make up your mind whether you want one large or several smaller focaccia, place on a well-oiled (with olive oil) baking sheet, cover with a damp cloth, and let it rise until doubled in bulk. Bake in a fairly hot, 400°F, oven for nearly 30 minutes, or until nicely browned. Serve hot or warm.

That is how it all got started, and we'll give the credit to the Genoese. But, of course, the Genoese weren't the only ones making this kind of thing. Similar flavored breads show up other places, sometimes with different names.

Naturally, the more astute among you detected that good ol' #1 recipe: the primo bread. It seems that often, with these good Italian bread recipes, the basic dough is made first, and the oil is added afterward. This allows the yeast to develop with little or no interference from the fat (the shortening or oil). As the dough ripens, it is stronger, and will work better with virtually anything you put into it.

I started this section with foccacia because the word sounds kind of nice and it is ridiculously easy. If you make this thing, people will be singing your praises, calling you a gourmet cook, and other things. You can make even smaller loaves — rolls, as it were — and have those dandy sandwiches, or a *pan bagnat,* of olde Euro lore. While the bread is still warm, slice it horizontally and spread olive oil on it; then add whatever — black or green olives, garlic, onions, tomatoes, et cetera, including radishes, cucumbers, sweet peppers or pepperocini, capers, and sliced hard-boiled egg.

Mrs. Wanless' Garlic Bread

Let's go a step further: Using the Focaccia recipe to start, instead of the more time-consuming second step of adding the oil and herbs, do this: Pour ¼ cup of good fragrant olive oil into a couple of 9-inch cake pans and put in a couple (3, 4, 5, it depends upon your garlic tolerance) cloves of garlic, and, if you have some, fresh rosemary, a good-sized sprig of it (or the dried stuff). Heat the oil with the herbs in it until it is really fragrant, but don't let the garlic get brown. When the oil is really fragrant, take it off the heat and strain it, let it cool to just lukewarm, and then roll out the dough to a round, flat disc (or 2 or 3, or several round discs), and then lay them in the oil. Let the discs rise for an hour in a warm place. Bake in a 400°F oven for 15 to 20 minutes.

Pizza

That's right! All of this invariably leads up to pizza. There is little I can add to the already vast literature of pizza. My job is to make it easier. Let me make a couple of suggestions:

1. Putting quarry tiles on the rack in your oven will contribute to a better pizza and crisper crust. Six will usually do it, and they are very inexpensive.

2. High temperatures (450°F and higher) also contribute to a superior pizza. So, back to old #1:

> 4 C flour
>
> 1¼ C warm water
>
> 2 tsp salt
>
> 1 tsp yeast
>
> <u>Optional:</u>
>
> 1 T honey or brown sugar
>
> 1 to 2 tsp olive oil

Adding a tablespoon of honey or brown sugar to the above helps the flavor a bit and helps it to brown better. Adding the olive oil after the dough has been made and risen the first time (see Focaccia recipe) gives the bread a crisper crust. If you can, let the dough age a day or two in the fridge.

When you're ready to bake, try this vastly simpler version (but only when fresh, real tomatoes are available).

When you've worked the oil (flavored or no) into the dough and spread the dough out, bake 10 minutes in a 450°F oven. Remove the pizza disc or platform and then slice a tomato, a plum tomato or whatever, in quarter-inch slices. Use one or two tomatoes, depending on the diameter of the pizza. Spread out a good thick layer of mozzarella cheese on the pizza disc; then place the tomato slices around in a nice, orderly fashion; place a basil leaf on each tomato slice and a garlic clove on each basil leaf. Do this gingerly or you'll burn your fingers. Then dribble a bead of olive oil on each of these little crowns. Put this back into the 450°F oven and bake another 5 minutes.

If it's wintertime and the only thing available are those tomatoes that are red on the outside and white on the inside and taste awful, spread a little leftover tomato sauce first, then the cheese, then whatever the spirit of cooking dictates. Another nice touch is to buy a can of diced or chopped tomatoes, warm them, saute some garlic, onions, and various and sundry Italian type herbs, stir in the tomato chunks, stir briefly, let cool a bit, and use this for the sauce base on the pizza.

Rolled Pizza

We saw this offering in Chicago. It's an easy one to figure out and do. So, for a change: Use the recipe for pizza dough given in the Pizza recipe on page 85. Roll out the dough into a reasonably well-shaped rectangle or square, spread with very thin coating of a dense tomato sauce, then your mozzarella, and cooked Italian sausage. Roll this up and fit it in a bread pan (or if you have one, try fitting it into a Pullman Loaf pan). Bake at 400°F for about 25 minutes. Remove and let sit for 10 minutes; then slice and serve. You may want to have a thick, spicy tomato sauce, or even a cheese sauce, to ladle over the slices.

Calzones

Calzones are cousins of pizza. Like pizza, the making of calzones varies from district to district, and even from person to person. Here are two versions.

Calzones #1

(Makes 12 to 15 little calzones)

> Refrigerated Dough #1 (page 61)
>
> olive oil and butter for preparation
>
> 1 C mild onions, chopped
>
> 1 small can anchovies
>
> capers
>
> black olives

1. Take Refrigerated Dough #1 from the fridge and press all the air out of it. Knead as much as ¼ C of olive oil into the dough. Roll it out to ½ inch thick. Cut the dough into 3-inch squares and set them on baking sheets. Let them rest while you:

2. Saute the onions in 2 T olive oil and 2 T butter until they are translucent, but not brown.

3. Put a spoonful of onions on each square. Put a bit of anchovies on each mound of onions, then 2 or 3 capers on each, and a couple of black olive halves. Dribble on a bit more olive oil; then fold the squares in half, pressing the edges down with a fork. Prick a few holes in the dough with a fork. Brush them with olive oil, and bake in a 450°F oven for 15 to 20 minutes. Dip in a nice, spicy tomato or cheese sauce.

Calzones #2

This recipe is virtually the same as Calzones #1, except you fry the little guys in 350°F deep fat for about 5 minutes. Dip in tomato or cheese sauce.

Bruschetta

Italian bread

½ dozen cloves of garlic, crushed

olive oil

basil

anchovies

What you are working with here is slices of good Italian bread. There seem to be as many variations of bruschetta as there are Italians (natural and wannabees) making it. So, where to start?

So you're going to watch *The Godfather* for the umpteenth time, and you want something quick and Italian to munch on? Take a nice loaf of fresh Italian bread. Slice it thick, one inch at least. Toast it in the oven until it is just getting crisp.

Perhaps you have someone coming over, and it's summer and you want to sit out on the balcony and munch something with your beer or wine. Try making an Italian loaf as a large round disc. Bake it on the quarry tiles in your oven. When done, let it cool a bit; then slice it horizontally. Put both pieces in the oven until they are just getting crisp.

Then you take a paste of a half-dozen cloves of garlic you have crushed, and spread it lightly but completely over the crumb side of those big round slices. Dribble a nice stream of good olive oil concentrically from the circumference to the center. You can sprinkle some fresh basil over this, but don't feel obligated to, and if you are really gutsy, add some chopped anchovies. You get the drift of this? That's right; some diced tomatoes wouldn't hurt. But the main thing is the garlic and the olive oil, because it is, after all, really just garlic bread.

Put these slices or discs back in the oven for a couple of minutes, to get them nice and hot. Eat them while drinking a nice dry zinfandel (the dark, dry, red stuff).

Stuffed Sandwich Loaf

What about a real meal in a loaf? First you take a loaf of bread. It can be either one baked in the bread machine or a free-formed loaf baked in the oven. You will want some aluminum foil. You will need:

8 slices of bacon (or ¼ lb of prosciutto, or even cooked ham)

⅔ C chopped onions

2 cloves of garlic, chopped

1 small can of artichoke hearts, drained and chopped

½ C grated parmesan cheese*

⅓ C mayonnaise

¼ C minced fresh parsley

¼ tsp freshly ground pepper

*Better to buy the wedges of parmesan cheese and shred it than to buy it grated.

For the sauce:

a clove or two of garlic, chopped

⅓ C dry white wine

16-oz can of tomato sauce

1. Cut the top quarter off the loaf of bread.

2. Hollow out the bottom three-fourths of the loaf by removing the white part, and take the white out of the top, leaving about a half-inch of crust. Cut the bread that you removed into small bits.

3. Cut the bacon into one-inch pieces and cook until almost crisp. Drain on a paper towel.

4. Save one or 2 T of the bacon fat, and saute the onions and 2 cloves of garlic until translucent (3 to 4 minutes) in it. If you are using the other ham products, use olive oil instead.

5. Combine the bread bits, bacon (or ham), the artichokes, mayonnaise, half the parsley, most of the cheese (reserve 2 T of the cheese), and fill the cavity of the bread shell with the mixture.

6. Put the top back on the loaf, wrap it in aluminum foil, and bake at 375°F for 25 minutes.

7. While the loaf is baking, saute the remaining two cloves of garlic in oil for a minute or two, add the remaining parsley, and then the can of tomato sauce. Bring to a low boil; then simmer for 10 minutes. Add the white wine and remainder of the cheese, and simmer for another 5 minutes.

If you've done this right, the loaf and the sauce should be done at the same time.

8. Remove the loaf, slice it in 1-inch slices, serve on a plate, and ladle a nice bit of sauce over it.

Cake Recipes for Machines with a Cake Setting

Introduction to Cakes

In the other chapters there are several recipes that might best be described as cake recipes — the Moravian Sugar Cake and the Pandolce Genovese, to mention two. They are wonderful things, but they are not what most of us think of as cake. Many, if not most, of the newer bread machines have what they call a cake setting or cycle. The recipe books which come with these machines tell us (in effect) to dump a box of cake mix into the bread pan, select the cake setting, start the machine, and away you go. Some of the books also supply you with a recipe or two for what we used to call a "dump cake." You may remember those simple, single-bowl, quick cakes which were popular for a while. Now, let's make no mistake about this: the cakes which the machines produce are not what we normally think of cakes: light, fluffy, high. These are simple, you might say, junk cakes supreme — sweet, moist, a bit heavy — but they are good cakes, nonetheless, and if you spread them with enough icing, they'll fill the bill (and the belly), and do it in only about 5 minutes of your valuable time and in most cases without messing up any other bowls.

I was asked if I could come up with some recipes for the people whose machines have the cake cycle and who might be interested in trying something a little different. My wife, Holly, who did most of the research and testing for this chapter, quickly jumped on this, and immediately adapted one of her favorite cake recipes to the cake cycle. This was one of those dump cakes, a chocolate cake which called for mixing all the ingredients in the same pan in which you baked the cake. When we had a houseful of kids, this was the best way to ensure a dessert when there was no time for making one — perfect for the bread machine.

We have two bread machines that are totally different, but both have a cake setting. One has the more common bread machine pan, which I call a vertical pan. And we have a newish machine which has a horizontal pan (and two kneader paddles). With these two basic types of machines, there is a problem which arises at the outset. The two different-sized pans have bases with different areas, what architects call their footprint. I mean that while both machines are maximum 2½-lb loaf machines, the horizontal pan has a larger footprint. The horizontal pan's base is approximately 42 square inches, while the vertical pan's is about 27 square inches. The recommended capacities for flour and liquid for the cake setting of both machines is about the same. The end result seems to be that the cakes that come out of the machines with the vertical pan are squat and square, about 4 inches high. Those which come from the machines with the horizontal pans look like loaf cakes and are about the same height. The horizontal pan gives the batter more room to rise, and this produces a somewhat lighter cake.

We've checked the recipes we came up with in both machines and, aside from some differences, the products are equally good. Where there is potentially a serious difference, I've included two sizes for recipes, a somewhat smaller one for the square-bottomed pan.

Since my wife, Holly, did most of the preparation for this chapter, I thought it was fair to have her add a word or two. She notes:

"When you are converting your own recipes to fit the bread maker on the cake setting, keep in mind both the shape of the loaf and the capacity. A rule of thumb is that if your recipe calls for a loaf pan, it is definitely a good candidate for the bread maker; if it calls for a 9 inch × 13 inch pan or two 9-inch cake pans, cut the recipe in half. The measurement of flour in these recipes is done with unsifted flour. If you are sifting the dry ingredients to mix them together, do it after measuring.

"To reap the benefits of this time-saving method of making cakes, you may have to use your imagination to turn the result into a dessert perfect for company, particularly if you have a machine with a vertical pan. The chocolate cake is a case in point. When we tried it, the cake itself looked like a large, squat brownie (but it tasted incredible). By the time it was sliced, filled and iced, it looked like one of those fancy desserts you can buy in a good bakery. Since you have saved so much time making the cake itself, you have a little extra time to dress it up; and really that's the fun part of baking.

"Besides the size of the machine, you must also keep in mind that you are using kneader paddles rather than a mixer to beat the cake. Don't get me wrong, those short paddles do a surprisingly thorough job of beating the cake, but they do have limitations, notably in beating the shortening, because the lumps work their way to the top of the other ingredients and stay there. To get around this, with butter, we put it into the microwave for 20 seconds on high before adding it. This softened it without melting it. With solid shortening, we put the shortening in first, gradually adding the sugar; then we added each of the eggs.

"All cake recipes tell you to have the ingredients at room temperature. In the case of the bread maker, if you are using either solid shortening or butter, this is doubly important. You can always put the eggs in hot water for a few minutes to bring the temperature up and put the milk into the microwave for a few seconds."

Our two different bread machines with cake settings have warning beepers to let you know when to add ingredients. My Zojirushi actually stops to accommodate this; the other machine just keeps going. So, what you want to do, with all of the machines, I think, is as follows: when the machine beeps, simply add what needs to be added. We work with this feature rather a lot, sometimes creaming shortening and sugar, sometimes making sure the liquids are well-mixed before adding the rest of the ingredients.

The following is rather important also: After you've added the dry ingredients, stir them with a narrow rubber spatula, even if the machine is continuing to mix. You want to get any dry ingredients sticking to the sides, bottom, or the corners of the pan.

The kneader paddles in bread machines, I've noticed, have a tendency to have the nonstick surface beaten off them. The hard wheat and various other ingredients we put in the machines makes this inevitable. Since the cakes are only baked in the machines, unlike the yeast-risen bread, which is often removed as dough and baked in pans in the oven, what do you do to stop the cake batter from sticking to a kneader paddle that has suffered the loss of its nonstick surface? My wife suggests: as soon as the machine stops mixing and is paused before going on to the bake cycle, reach into the bread pan and pull the paddle, or paddles, out of the machine. It's a gooey, sticky job. To make this paddle removal a bit easier, put some cooking oil or margarine on the paddle shaft before putting the paddle on it. Then, of course, you just let your machine do its job.

Beginning at the beginning, I suppose it makes sense to start our recipes with the one next. This is almost ridiculously simple for a cake; but then, that's what the bread machine is all about.

A Good Old Basic Cake

½ C milk

2 eggs

½ C soft butter (or half butter, half margarine)

1 tsp vanilla

Dry ingredients:

1¾ C cake or pastry flour

1 C sugar

2 tsp baking powder

½ tsp salt

Have all ingredients at room temperature. Mix or sift the dry ingredients together. Set aside. Add the ingredients in the order given, with the dry last.

Icing

2 T butter (or salt-free margarine, or vegetable shortening)

1¼ C confectioners' sugar

¼ tsp salt

1 tsp vanilla (or rum, brandy, or any tasty cordial)

What do you put on this cake? Icing, of course. No, not that canned stuff. Here is how you — or better yet, one of your kids, maybe even your husband or your wife — make a nice butter cream icing, sufficient, at least, for the above cake. You'll need a mixer. Begin beating the butter. Gradually begin to add to the bowl the confectioners' sugar and salt. When the sugar is blended, pour in, while beating, the vanilla or other flavoring; mix until blended, a minute or so. Cut the cake in half horizontally, and carefully (because of the crumbs) spread the icing on the bottom layer. Put the top layer on it, and spread the rest of the icing all over the cake. Lick the bowl and the spreader carefully. I just love cake.

Coffee Cake

Yes. You may serve it with tea. You'll note the Streusel topping.

¼ C butter

⅓ C sugar

1 egg

½ tsp vanilla

⅔ C milk

1½ C flour

2 tsp baking powder

¼ tsp salt

For Streusel Topping:

1 T flour

1 T sugar

2 T butter

¼ to ½ tsp lemon juice

½ tsp cinnamon

All ingredients should be at warm room temperature. Select the cake cycle. Make sure the butter is very soft; you might even want to warm it in the microwave. Spread it on the bottom of the bread pan. Next, spread the sugar over the butter.

Start the machine. Let it run a minute or two, to cream the two ingredients. Now add the egg and the vanilla; then the milk. Sift the rest of the dry ingredients together and add to the pan. If your machine has one of those loaf type pans, kind of spread the dry ingredients over the other ingredients as you add them. Use a narrow rubber spatula to move the dry ingredients off the sides and out of the corners of the pan.

Mix the streusel topping ingredients together in a separate container. After cake has baked about 15 minutes, open the machine and spread the topping on. Careful! It's hot in there! Now you just let the machine do its job. When done, remove the cake. Eat hot.

Brown Sugar Cake

This is, like the basic cake, ridiculously simple, and equally good.

⅔ C milk

2 eggs

⅓ C soft butter, margarine, or shortening

1 tsp vanilla

1¾ C cake or pastry flour

¾ C brown sugar

3 tsp baking powder

¼ tsp salt

Have all ingredients at room temperature. Add the ingredients in the order above, and start the machine. We don't spread icing on this cake, but rather pour the topping over slices of it. It is that good old basic Lemon Sauce.

Lemon Sauce

1 T cornstarch

½ C sugar

1 T grated lemon rind

pinch of salt

1 C water

2 T lemon juice

2 T butter

Mix together the cornstarch, sugar, lemon rind, and salt. Cooking this over low heat in a saucepan, gradually add the water, while stirring constantly. Then cook this carefully over a medium–low heat, stirring it occasionally, for about 5 minutes. Then add the lemon juice and the butter; mix it well; and pour it over slices of the cooled cake. It is sooo good.

Apple Cake

I like it better without the nuts and raisins. Then it is just as the name says it is. But it also is good with the nuts and raisins.

> 1 egg
>
> ½ tsp vanilla
>
> ½ C oil
>
> 1 C flour
>
> ¾ C sugar
>
> ½ tsp cinnamon
>
> ½ tsp salt
>
> **5 minutes before the end of mixing, add:**
>
> 1 C thinly sliced apples (peeled)
>
> ½ C chopped walnuts
>
> ¼ C raisins

Have all ingredients at room temperature. Simply add the egg through salt ingredients to the bread pan in order listed. Select the cake setting; then at the beeper, or 5 minutes before the end of the mixing cycle, add the apples, walnuts, and raisins.

Blueberry Cake

If blueberries aren't in season, you can use frozen blueberries, but let them thaw first. A few hours out of the freezer, sitting on a plate, should do it.

½ C butter (softened)

1 C sugar

1 egg

1 C milk

2 C flour

4 tsp baking powder

½ tsp salt

At the beeper or 5 minutes before the end of mixing, add:

1 C blueberries

1 tsp lemon juice

1 tsp cinnamon

Have all ingredients at room temperature. Select the cake cycle. Take very soft butter (you might even want to give it a shot in the microwave, 20 to 30 seconds on high, depending upon just how cold the butter is), and spread it on the bottom of the bread pan. Then pour the sugar evenly over the butter.

Start the machine. Let it run a minute or two, to cream the two ingredients. During that time, stir the dry ingredients together and set aside.

Now add the egg, then the milk, to the bread pan. Then add the dry ingredients. If your machine has an addition beeper, add the blueberries when it beeps, along with the lemon juice and cinnamon. If your machine doesn't have a beeper, wait until the last 3 to 5 minutes of the stirring cycle before adding the berries. You don't want those berries ground up with the other stuff.

Just let the machine do its job. When done, remove the cake. It is best to serve this cake with heaping gobs of whipped cream.

Holly's Grandmother's Hickory Nut Cake

Fred Crissman, Holly's dad, now a spry 86 and moving right along, has been asking for this cake for years. Holly couldn't find a recipe for it. She finally did, written on the back of an envelope and stuck in her grandmother's old cookbook. The envelope was postmarked, 7:30 PM, July 3, 1923, Altoona, Pennsylvania (and had a 2-cent stamp still on it). Holly had to reduce the recipe by about one-third, because of the size limitations of the bread machine. Hickory nuts are a little hard to come by these days. Holly substituted pecans, which apparently even Fred's mother was inclined to do.

Dad says that these bread machine gadgets are getting you awfully close to the original loaves, because of the consistency of temperature maintained in these little "ovens." The temperature in modern home ovens can vary as much as 50 degrees as the thermostat strives to maintain temperature. Those old cast-iron stoves — wood-, coal-, or even gas-fired — retained their heat.

⅓ C butter (very soft)	1 C sugar
2 eggs	⅔ C milk
½ tsp vanilla	1¾ C flour
½ tsp baking powder	½ tsp salt

5 minutes before the end of mixing, add:

¾ C hickory nuts or pecans, chopped the size of raisins

¼ C flour

Have all ingredients at room temperature. Spread the butter on the bottom of the bread pan; then spread the sugar over the butter. Add the eggs, then the milk and vanilla. Sift together the flour, baking powder, and salt, and then sift all over the other ingredients in the bread pan. Start the machine. Mix the quarter-cup of flour with the nuts. When the machine beeps (or about 5 minutes before the end of the mixing cycle), add the nuts/flour mixture. Use a spatula to move all the dry ingredients off the sides of the pan, and out of the corners of the pan. Let the machine do its job. When done, remove the cake loaf from the pan.

Carrot Cake

Here's still another stalwart recipe, conveniently adapted to the cake setting of the bread machine. Because of the nature of the cake, it is not a high-riser. For the two different types of bread pans — the square-bottomed vertical and the elongated loaf pan — I am giving two recipes, a small one for the square-bottomed pan, and a large one for the other.

Recipe #1: Small Carrot Cake
(for square-bottomed pan)

2 eggs	½ C + 1½ tsp oil
1½ C grated carrots	1 C flour
1 C sugar	½ tsp baking soda
½ tsp salt	½ tsp cinnamon

Select the cake setting. Put the eggs, oil, and carrots into the pan and start the machine. Let it run a minute or so to mix the wet ingredients well. In a separate container, mix well or sift the dry ingredients together, and add to the machine. Remove cake when done. When cool, coat with the wonderful frosting.

Frosting for Carrot Cake

3 oz cream cheese	½ stick (2 oz) unsalted butter
1¾ C confectioners' sugar	1 tsp vanilla

Beat together these 4 ingredients until soft, fluffy, and ready to spread. This will coat either cake nicely.

Recipe #2. Large Carrot Cake
(for loaf-pan style machine)

4 eggs	1 C + 1 T oil
3 C grated carrots	2 C flour
2 C sugar	1 tsp baking soda
1 tsp salt	1 tsp cinnamon

Select the cake setting. Put the eggs, oil, and carrots into the pan and start the machine. Let it run a minute or so to mix the wet ingredients well. In a separate container, mix well or sift the dry ingredients together, and add to the machine. Remove cake when done and, when cool, coat with frosting.

White Forest Chocolate Cake

The Zojirushi owner's manual has a mouth-watering picture of a chocolate cake baked in their machine. They call it a Black Forest Cake. The cake is sliced into 3 layers, lavishly spread with chocolate icing inside and out, and topped with cherries. The instructions call for spreading it with chocolate icing from a can. We don't use mixes (just ornery, I guess) and certainly wouldn't use icing from a can! Humph!

This is Holly's answer to the question: How does one prepare a fancy, elegant dessert without spending much time? This looks marvelous, tastes better. She got the name as a play on the Black Forest Cake name. Holly's icing (see page 103) is white.

½ C hot coffee + 1 tsp baking soda	½ C milk
1 egg	¼ C oil
½ tsp vanilla	1 C flour
1 C sugar	⅓ C + 1 T cocoa
½ tsp baking powder	½ tsp salt

<u>For between the layers:</u>

¼ to ½ C cherry preserves or jelly

shot of brandy (1 oz)

Have all ingredients at room temperature. Select the cake setting. Add all the liquid ingredients to the bread pan first, and start it. In a separate container, mix or sift the dry ingredients together and add them to the bread pan. Using a spatula, scrape the sides of the pan, and make sure the dry ingredients don't collect in the corners of the pan. Then let the machine do its job.

When the cake is done and cool, do the following:

1. To make layers, slice the cake in 3 even horizontal slices.

2. Take the cherry preserves, or cherry jelly, and warm it in the microwave (30 seconds on high should do it). Add the brandy to the cherry goody, and mix well. Spread the preserves on each layer, and on the top and sides as well. Holly is quick to add: "Don't feel limited to just cherry stuff; red currant jelly is equally good, as are raspberry preserves, black or red. If you want to use strawberries, rum is acceptable."

3. After the preserves have cooled on the cake, it has to be coated. Whipped cream comes to my mind, but then it always does. Holly uses the following, her adaptation of the icing for Red Velvet Cake.

White Forest Icing

1 C milk	4 T flour
1 C sugar	½ C butter or margarine
½ C vegetable shortening	½ tsp vanilla
pinch of salt	

In a saucepan, cook milk and flour until thick, stirring constantly over low heat. Allow to cool. Cream the sugar, butter, and shortening together. Add the thick flour mixture to the creamed butter mix; then the salt and vanilla. Beat this combination for about 10 minutes. It will be marvelously light and fluffy. Spread this on the cake. Don't expect leftovers, but this icing will keep for quite a while.

Maple Spice Cake

We use our own maple-flavored syrup in this cake; see recipe (page 105).

1 egg

¼ C of our maple-flavored syrup

¼ C oil or melted shortening

½ C sour milk*

1½ C flour

½ tsp baking soda

½ C sugar

½ tsp salt

5 minutes before end of mixing cycle, add:

¾ tsp cinnamon

¼ tsp ground cloves

½ C chopped walnuts

*You sour milk by adding 1 tsp vinegar or lemon juice to ½ C milk.

All ingredients should be at room temperature. Start by selecting the cake cycle. Put the wet ingredients into the pan, put the pan into the machine, and start the machine. Let it run a minute or two, mixing the ingredients thoroughly. Mix or sift the baking soda, sugar, and salt in a separate bowl; then add the bread pan. Use a spatula to push the ingredients away from the corners. Either at the beeper or 5 minutes before the end of the stirring cycle, depending upon the type of machine you have, add the cinnamon, cloves, and walnuts into the pan. Use a spatula to make sure all the dry ingredients are off the sides, and out of the corners of the pan. When done, remove from the pan.

Maple-Flavored Syrup

1 C boiling water	1 C brown sugar
1 C white sugar	½ tsp vanilla
½ tsp maple flavoring	¼ C real maple syrup

Stir the brown and white sugar into the boiling water. Boil on high, stirring occasionally, until clear. Remove from heat. Let settle for 5 minutes; then add the vanilla and maple flavoring, and real maple syrup. This makes a good imitation, which is far better than that sticky syrup on the store shelves and less than half the cost.

Breads or Loaves for Machines with a Cake Setting

These breads are, after all, savory cakes; like cakes, their leaven is derived mainly from acid that produces carbon dioxide and raises the whole content of the ingredients, rather than the same carbon dioxide pushing against glutinous "threads," as in yeast breads. The quick breads we included are good, and at least one is sensational. They are tender and actually almost better the next day. That's true of the cakes also, but in our house no cake has been around long enough to give scientific evidence.

Banana Bread*

Here is another stalwart recipe, conveniently adapted to the cake setting of the bread machine.

½ C vegetable shortening

1¼ C sugar

2 eggs

1 tsp vanilla

¼ C sour milk**

1 C mashed bananas (3 medium or 2 large)

2 C flour

½ tsp baking soda

1 tsp baking powder

¾ tsp salt

5 minutes before the end of mixing, add:

1 C broken pecans (optional)

For topping: ½ C slivered almonds

*Or: why one waits for the bananas to get black. Remember: the darker, the sweeter.
**A squirt of lemon or vinegar will sour it.

Have all ingredients at room temperature. Select the cake setting. Put the shortening and sugar into the pan and start the machine. Let it run a minute or so to cream the butter and sugar. Add the eggs, the vanilla, the sour milk, and then the bananas. Mix well or sift the flour, baking soda, baking powder, and salt together, and add to the bread pan as it mixes. At the beeper, or 5 minutes before the end of mixing, add the pecans, if you wish. Remove bread from pan when done and think about the following: You can turn this sensible, utilitarian bread into something wonderful by slicing it in half, or thirds, horizontally, and spreading Flavored Whipped Topping within it and on it when cool. Then sprinkle with slivered almonds.

Flavored Whipped Topping

2 C milk	3 T cornstarch
3 T flour	¼ tsp salt
⅓ C sugar	2 egg yolks, beaten
1 tsp vanilla	2 T butter or margarine
1 T rum or brandy (optional)	½ pint whipped cream

Scald 1½ C milk in a saucepan. Set aside. Mix together the cornstarch, flour, salt and sugar; add the remaining ½ cup of cold milk to make a paste. Gradually stir this mixture into the scalded milk; keep stirring constantly until it is thickened (this should take about 5 minutes). Stir a small amount (¼ cup, say) of the hot mixture into the egg yolks; then gradually add the egg yolk mixture to the whipped cream and rum or brandy. Continue cooking over a low heat for another 3 minutes. Remove from the heat and add the vanilla, and then the butter. Stir it in well, and let it cool.

Orange Bread/Cake

This recipe is for 3 cakes in one. If you put in the optionals, it becomes an almost totally different cake, in flavor and texture. My daughter Kirsten suggested option #2. The first two ways, it is equally good done for breakfast and served hot, with lots of butter. Make it tonight, and serve it cool tomorrow, as a luncheon treat, thinly sliced with cream cheese spread upon it. Kirsten's way, spread with a chocolate sauce, it is an elegant dessert.

2 T very soft margarine

1 egg

grated rind (the zest) of one juice orange

¼ C orange juice

½ C milk

1 T orange marmalade

1½ C flour

⅔ C sugar

2 tsp baking powder

½ tsp salt

Option #1: 5 minutes before end of mixing, add:

⅛ tsp ground cloves

½ tsp cinnamon

½ C chopped pecans

¼ C golden raisins

Option #2: Five minutes before end of mixing, add:

1 C miniature chocolate chips

Have all ingredients at room temperature. Select the cake setting. Put the wet ingredients, including margarine, into the pan. Start the machine. After a minute or two, add the rest of the ingredients.

If you choose one of the options, add them at the beeper, or 5 minutes before the end of the mixing. Remove cake when done and enjoy.

Raisin-Walnut Bread

You've probably seen a variation of this recipe before. We have 3 of those church cookbooks; a variation of it is in each of them. Why not? It's a good recipe. Here it is, adapted to the bread machine.

1 C boiling water	¼ C butter (soft)
¾ C sugar	1 egg
2 C flour	1 tsp baking soda
½ tsp salt	

5 minutes before the end of mixing, add:

1 C broken walnuts

2 C raisins

Have all ingredients at room temperature. Pour the boiling water over the raisins and let sit until warm; add the butter to the raisins to soften. Select the cake setting. Put the sugar, the egg, then the hot water from the raisins in the pan, and start the machine. Now add the flour, baking soda, and salt. At the beeper, or 5 minutes before the end of the mixing cycle, add the raisins and walnuts.

Basic Gingerbread

This rather basic gingerbread is supplied in two sizes, one for the square-bottomed bread pans, the larger size for the loaf pan. Gingerbread is a requisite with bean soup.

Small Gingerbread (square bread pan)

⅓ C butter (very soft)

⅔ C brown sugar (packed)

1 egg

⅓ C sour milk or buttermilk*

⅓ C molasses mixed with ⅛ C boiling water

2 C flour

1½ tsp powdered ginger

⅛ tsp ground cloves or allspice

⅛ tsp nutmeg or mace

1¼ tsp baking soda

½ tsp salt

*You can sour milk by putting a teaspoon of lemon juice, or vinegar, into the milk.

All ingredients should be at warm room temperature. Choose the cake cycle. Using very soft butter (you might even want to give it a shot in the microwave; 20 to 30 seconds, depending upon just how cold the butter is, on high), spread it on the bottom of the bread pan; then pour the sugar evenly over the butter. Start the machine. Let it run a minute or two, to cream the two ingredients. During that time, stir the dry ingredients together in a separate container, but don't add yet.

Add the egg, then the milk, and the water and molasses. Now add the dry ingredients. Use a spatula to make sure all the dry ingredients are out of the corner of the pan and off the sides of it. Let the machine do its job. When done, remove the bread.

Large Gingerbread (loaf-shaped bread pan)

¼ C butter (very soft)

1 C brown sugar (packed)

1 egg

½ C sour milk or buttermilk*

½ C molasses mixed with ¼ C (scant) boiling water

2¼ C flour

2 tsp powdered ginger

¼ tsp ground cloves or allspice

¼ tsp nutmeg or mace

1½ tsp baking soda

½ tsp salt

Follow same procedures as for small gingerbread.

Fancy Gingerbread

This recipe was outlandish, even for me. I have made an attempt to civilize it, tailoring it, somewhat, to fit the bread machines. If you must make this in a square, vertical type bread pan, add the teaspoon of yeast that is indicated as an option. The dough hasn't the strength to climb the walls of the pan as it is. This is a good holiday-season cake, served late in the evening, with grog or a Tom and Jerry; maybe just with port or brandy — and in small pieces. It is rich.

½ C butter	½ C brown sugar
2 eggs	⅔ C molasses
⅓ C orange juice	⅓ C brandy
2¼ C flour	2 tsp powdered ginger
1 tsp cream of tartar	1 tsp baking soda
½ tsp salt	

5 minutes before end of mixing, add:

¾ C chopped candied ginger

¾ C golden raisins

¾ C shopped almonds

All ingredients should be at warm room temperature. Either heat the molasses or the orange juice in the microwave and mix the two. This makes the molasses blend better with the other ingredients. Select the cake cycle. Using very soft butter, spread it on the bottom of the bread pan; then pour the sugar evenly over. Start the machine. Let it run a minute or two, to cream the butter and sugar. During that time, stir the flour, ginger, cream of tartar, baking soda, and salt together. Add the egg; then the orange juice, brandy, and molasses. Now add the dry ingredients. Using a spatula, make sure all the dry ingredients are out of the corner of the pan and off the sides of it.

If your machine has an addition beeper, when it beeps add the ginger, raisins, and almonds. If your machine doesn't have a beeper, wait until the last 3 to 5 minutes of the stirring cycle before adding them. Now just let the machine do its job. When done, remove from the pan.

Brown Bread

Well, of course it can't be *that* brown bread. That brown bread, Boston Brown Bread, steams for sometimes a couple of hours. But this is worth a try, if you like brown bread.

½ C dark molasses mixed with ¼ C (scant) boiling water

1 T very soft butter

1 egg

1 C sour milk or buttermilk

½ C dark brown sugar

1¼ C whole wheat flour

½ C flour

¼ C cornmeal

1½ tsp baking soda

½ tsp salt

5 minutes before end of mixing, add:

½ C raisins

Select the cake setting. Mix well, or sift, the dry ingredients together in a separate container. Put the ingredients into the pan in the order above and start machine. Add the raisins at the beeper, or 5 minutes before the end of the mixing. Remove the bread when done. Serve cool with cream cheese.

Light Brown or Golden Brown Bread

This is light-colored brown bread, not low-calorie brown bread, as you will shortly see. This is a happy accident. As I was trying to develop a bread-machine version of brown bread, I accidentally came up with this. It was so good, I decided to include it.

½ C dark corn syrup mixed with ¼ C (scant) boiling water

1 T very soft butter or margarine

1 egg

1 C sour milk or buttermilk

½ C brown sugar

¼ C whole wheat flour

¼ C cornmeal

1¼ C all-purpose flour

1½ tsp baking soda

½ tsp salt

5 minutes before the end of mixing, add:

½ C golden raisins

Select the cake setting. Mix well, or sift, the dry ingredients together in a separate container. Put the ingredients into the bread machine pan in the order listed above, and start machine. Add the raisins at the beeper, or 5 minutes before the end of the mixing. Remove the bread when done. Serve cool with cream cheese.

Beer Bread

10 oz beer	1 T oil
¼ C sugar	3 C self-rising or all-purpose flour*
1 T baking powder	1½ tsp salt

*If you use self-rising flour, omit the baking powder and salt.

Pour the beer and oil into the bread pan. The oil is needed to smooth out the texture. Mix the rest of the ingredients together. If yours is a horizontal, loaf bread pan, spread the dry ingredients more or less evenly over the beer. (For the other style of breadmaker, I suggest using the Porter Bread recipe.) Select cake cycle and let the machine run. Serve hot or, even better, grilled in butter and olive oil.

Herb Beer Bread

10 oz beer	1 T oil
2½ C self-rising* or all-purpose flour	½ C cornmeal
1 T baking powder	1 tsp salt
1½ tsp Italian seasoning	

Optional: At beeper or 5 minutes before the end of mixing, add:

sun-dried tomatoes

black olives

onions

other nutritious scraps

*If you use self-rising flour, omit the baking powder and salt.

Pour the beer and oil into the bread pan. Mix the dry ingredients together. Spread the dry ingredients evenly over the beer. Select the cake cycle and start. At the beeper, or 5 minutes before the end of the mix cycle, add the sun-dried tomatoes, etc. if you wish. Serve sliced hot, or, even better, grilled in butter and olive oil or put under the broiler for two minutes. A full-flavored bread.

Basic Cornbread

Cornbread, that necessity with chili, fried fish, or chicken. It has been around for probably as long as the basic bread recipe. Like the basic bread recipe, each time you taste it, it's like the first time. How handy that it can be made nicely in the bread machine. Cornbread is scrumptious hot and only a little less so cold. If you are fortunate enough to have some left over, the next morning you can slice it thinly and grill it; then it is back to scrumptious again.

1 C milk	1 egg
¼ C shortening	1 C yellow cornmeal
1 C flour	3 tsp baking powder
¼ C sugar	1 tsp salt

All ingredients should be at warm room temperature. Select the cake cycle. Put the wet ingredients into the pan (including the shortening); put the pan into the machine, and start the machine. Let it run a minute or two, mixing the ingredients thoroughly. During that time, stir the dry ingredients together in a separate container. Add the dry ingredients, depending upon the type of machine you have, either at the beeper, or five minutes before the end of the stirring cycle. Use a spatula to make sure all the dry ingredients are out of the corners of the pan and off the sides. Let the machine do its job. When done, remove the cornbread.

Guadalajara Cornbread

This is the Basic Cornbread taken several steps further. It is scrumptious hot, and only a little less so cold. Have some left over so you can slice it thin and grill it; then on each slice, put a slice of tomato, a poached egg with a slice of Canadian bacon or regular bacon on either side, and put a scoop of salsa on the plate; then it is back to scrumptious again.

1 C milk	2 eggs
3 T olive oil	1 C yellow cornmeal
1 C flour	3 tsp baking powder
1 T sugar	1 tsp salt

5 minutes before the end of mixing, add:

½ C corn kernels (fresh, canned or frozen)

¼ C diced green chilis

¼ C onions

¼ C chopped olives

½ C shredded cheddar cheese

All ingredients should be at warm room temperature. Select the cake cycle. Put the wet ingredients into the pan, the pan into the machine, and start the machine. Let it run a minute or two, mixing the ingredients thoroughly. During that time stir the dry ingredients together in a separate container and then add. Use a spatula to make sure all the dry ingredients are out of the corners and off the sides of the pan. Depending upon the type of machine you have, at the beeper or 5 minutes before the end of the stirring cycle, add the corn, chilis, onions, olives, and cheese. Let the machine do its job. When done, remove the cornbread.

Make this loaf Saturday night for Sunday brunch. A nice fruity white wine would go very well with this.

Some Interesting Things to Do with Bread Dough

An Edible Bread Bowl

This really isn't all that hard to do, if you have the right size bowls. I have nesting stainless steel bowls 10 inches and 11 inches in diameter. I made a recipe that accommodates these pans. You can modify to fit yours.

1 C water	3 C all-purpose flour
1 T lard	2 tsp sugar
2 tsp salt	1 tsp yeast

Do this on the dough cycle. Remove when done; place in an ungreased bowl; cover with plastic wrap; and chill for an hour or so.

When you are ready to make the bowl, spray the bottom surface of the smaller bowl with cooking oil, all the way to the edges, so the dough won't stick anywhere. Also spray the inside of the larger bowl the same way. I use a professional cooking spray, a food-grade silicon spray, but you can use a cooking oil spray. You don't want too much grease on either surface, or it will be too slippery. All you want is for the dough not to stick to the surfaces.

Roll out the dough into a large circle, sufficient to cover the smaller of the two bowls completely. Place that circle of dough over the inverted smaller bowl and put it on a baking sheet. Invert the larger bowl over the dough on the smaller bowl. Press it down firmly. Put a heavy weight (I use an iron frying pan) on the top bowl. Let this sit for 15 minutes while you heat the oven to 400°F. Put this strange-looking thing in the oven and bake about 15 minutes.

Remove from the oven and take off the weight and the upper bowl carefully — it is going to be hot! Put the bowl with the dough back into the oven for another 10 minutes. Take the bread bowl out of the oven again, and remove the inner bowl. Set the bread bowl upright on the baking sheet. You'll want a nice shiny finish, so brush the inside with an egg wash, if you have one handy, or just with some milk. Put the bread bowl back in the oven for another 5 minutes. It should be done. Doesn't that look great?

You can use the bowl as something to put rolls in; when the rolls are all gone, you can eat the bowl. Or you can use it as a very interesting salad bowl. Or you can shellac it, and use it again and again.

After having made the above, I began to wonder — what if my dear readers didn't have nesting stainless steel bowls? Then I remembered that my youngest daughter, Simone, found a recipe in a children's cookbook and made an honest-to-goodness chili bowl. She did this by simply following the instructions that said to drape flattened pizza dough over a soup bowl. So, you don't have nesting bowls? Simply drape the dough noted in the recipe above over a large ovenproof bowl and bake as noted above (except you won't have to remove the frying pan and covering bowl). You will want to remove the bread bowl in the last 5 to 10 minutes, brush with milk or egg wash, and put it back in the oven right-side up to bake for the remaining time. It won't be as thin and crispy as the first bread bowl, but it will be good, really good.

How about using the bread bowl to put a good spinach dip in and eat the dip with? Here's a recipe for a good spinach dip.

Spinach Dip

2 packages of frozen chopped spinach (about 20 oz total), defrosted	1 pt good sour cream
	4 oz feta cheese
½ C good olive oil	¼ C white vinegar
½ tsp ground mustard	½ C good fresh real bacon bits
½ tsp freshly ground black pepper	½ tsp salt

Mix together well. Put in the above-mentioned bowl. Break off pieces of the bowl and dip in the dip.

Dipping Bread

I came up with this while developing the edible bread bowl recipe. It was the answer to something I had wondered about for quite a while. Crackers! They are, to my way of thinking, hideously expensive, especially when you consider they have roughly the same ingredients as bread. So I've wondered about "bread crackers." Couldn't one make a crackerlike device for dipping in not only the above spinach dip, but perhaps in a really thick clam chowder? Of course one could! Using the recipe for the bread bowl (page 118), here's how:

Prepare dough in the bread machine on the dough cycle. Remove the dough when done, place in an ungreased bowl, cover with plastic wrap, and chill for at least an hour.

I use two pizza pans, 14 inches in diameter, but you can use a couple of cookie or baking sheets. First, spray the sheet thoroughly with cooking oil, all the way to the edges. Roll out the dough into a large circle (or oblong if you're using baking sheets). Place the rolled dough on the sheet or pan. Spray the bottom of the second pan or sheet with cooking oil. Place it on top of the dough. Press it down firmly. Place a heavy weight (e.g., an iron frying pan) onto the top sheet. Let this sit for 15 minutes while you heat the oven to 400°F. Bake 15 minutes. Remove from the oven and take off the weight and the upper sheet. Brush the top with water and sprinkle some coarse salt over the top. Put the big cracker back in the oven for another 10 minutes.

When done, let it cool on a rack for 20 minutes or so. You might want take a sharp knife and score the top in 1-inch cuts going one direction, and 2- to 3-inch cuts going the other before it cools. That will make it easier to break off dipping pieces.

APPENDIXES

New, Improved Bread Pudding

In my ever-continuing experimentation with ways to get rid of leftover bread, besides feeding it to the ever-increasing number of sea gulls who winter in the Harrisburg area, I have improved my bread pudding recipe. If you haven't tried my older one, I suppose it doesn't matter. If you have, try the new one; it's much better than the old.

3 C milk	⅓ to ½ C sugar
½ tsp salt	grated rind of ½ lemon
3 to 4 C bread cubes	3 eggs, separated
1 tsp vanilla	juice of ½ lemon
¼ C brandy	½ C raisins, chopped dates, and/or pecans

Heat the milk; add the sugar, salt, lemon rind, and bread cubes. Let soak in the large ovenproof glass bowl in which you will cook it.

Beat the egg yolks, adding the vanilla, lemon juice, and brandy. Add this mixture to the above, gently stirring with a fork. Then stir in the fruit. (You can make it without the fruit, but why?)

Beat the egg whites until soft peaks form, and gently fold them into the above.

Place the bowl in a pan of hot water; then set this in a 350°F oven and bake for about an hour. Stick a knife in the middle; if it comes out clean, the pudding is done. Let it cool a bit; then eat it.

Sourdough Starter

Sourdough was the leaven used in rougher times, on the farm, in the chuck wagons, in the mining, logging, and such camps, where yeast wasn't readily available. The "sots" (yeast or leaven) jar, as the starter was called, chiefly among the German–Americans, imparted a nice, rich, slightly sour flavor to bread. But the jars sometimes "went bad," causing bad feelings between the millers and the ladies who purchased from them. The ladies blamed the flour the millers sold them; the millers blamed the sots jars the ladies used at home.

Now I have it from good sources that when yeast became readily available, and also people started making yeast cakes at home, the good old sots jar went, and Fleischmann's and Red Star Yeast (to name just the two more famous) replaced it.

It is that sour flavor you occasionally want in your more rustic breads. Yeast can add that flavor, that flavor common to good bread and good beer, if it is allowed to ferment a bit longer. The good French or French - type bakeries start their loaves the night before, allowing for that fermentation and the flavoring.

You say that you still want to mess around with sourdough? Okay: tonight, before you go to bed, put the following in the bread pan of your machine:

¾ C warm (about 100°F) potato water*

1 generous tsp honey

½ tsp salt

1 (scant) tsp yeast

*Water in which you boiled your potatoes; or, if you forgot to save that water, put a tablespoon of instant potatoes in a cup of warm water.

Let that sit in the pan for 10 minutes or so. You want to get that yeast up and foaming.

Now, add:

1½ C unbleached white flour

½ C coarse-ground rye flour**

**You can use regular rye if that's all you have.

Put the pan in the machine, select the dough cycle, and go to bed. (Yes, it is all right to watch Letterman first.) Tomorrow morning, take the dough out of the machine. It should be pretty spongy, and smell it! Isn't that a nice, sour fragrance? Put the dough in one of those self-sealing storage bags, or a comparatively airtight container. Keep it in the bottom of the fridge. It will keep over a week. You can add a portion (say, a cup) of it to your various bread or roll recipes. If you are baking the bread in the machine, you'll want to reduce the initial quantity of the recipe by about a cup. Add that portion of my starter to the bread pan after the dough has been working 10 minutes or so, and you should end up with a nice sourdough whatever. That's all there is to it.

The Pullman Loaf and Pan: Another Word or Two

In the chapter on the Pullman loaves, I didn't go into much detail about the pan itself. You are probably familiar with good old sandwich bread, those rather long, square loaves of bread, thinly sliced, and designed for proper measurement, ease of handling, and the rapid assemblage of sandwiches. That basically is the Pullman loaf design.

I thought you might like to know how the pan works, and where you can get them. The newer Pullman loaf pans, manufactured by Chicago Bakeware and sold by Dura-ware, are coated with an unusual and frankly marvelous product called aluminum silica. It looks like high-gloss marine varnish, and is probably the ultimate nonstick surface.

James Beard, in his book *Beard on Bread,* suggests another way to achieve the Pullman effect without the Pullman pan. He put the dough in a regular-sized bread pan, and puts a flat metal cover on top (a conventional baking sheet will do). Then he placed a 2 × 4 × 8 inch basic red brick on top of that. (You use the brick because as the bread rises in the oven it is very strong.) Well, I tried his method and it didn't quite work. The rising dough pushed both the brick and the top off the pan. I guess I used two-brick dough. So that's what I recommend — two bricks. If you don't have, or can't find two red bricks, any heat-resistant object in the neighborhood of 10 lbs will do the trick — maybe one of your barbells?

When you are using the regular-sized pan you will have to use a smaller recipe than the several I included in the Pullman recipes; a 3 to 3½ cup (of flour) recipe will work. Don't forget to grease or spray not only the bread pan, but the underside (the side touching the bread) of the top cover.

METRIC TABLE
Inches to Centimeters

Inches	mm	cm	Inches	mm	cm
¼	6	0.6	7	178	17.8
½	13	1.3	8	203	20.3
1	25	2.5	9	229	22.9
2	51	5.1	10	254	25.4
4	102	10.2	15	381	38.1
5	127	12.7	18	457	45.7
6	152	15.2			

US LIQUID MEASURE EQUIVALENCIES* AND METRIC CONVERSIONS

1 cup = 8 fluid ounces	1 tablespoon = 3 teaspoons
1 cup = 16 tablespoons	1 tablespoon = 15 mL
1 cup = 48 teaspoons	1 teaspoon = 5 mL
1 cup = 236 mL	**Abbreviations**
4.2 cups = 1 L	C = cup
1 fluid ounce = 6 teaspoons	T = tablespoon
1 fluid ounce = 2 tablespoons	t = teaspoon
1 fluid ounce = 29.5 mL	oz = ounce

*These are also used for measuring flour and other dry ingredients in this book.

FAHRENHEIT TO CENTIGRADE TEMPERATURES

100°F = 37.7°C	350°F = 176.6°C
200°F = 93.3°C	400°F = 204.4°C
240°F = 115.5°C	450°F = 232.2°C
300°F = 148.8°C	500°F = 260°C

Index